First World War
and Army of Occupation
War Diary
France, Belgium and Germany

35 DIVISION
106 Infantry Brigade
Durham Light Infantry
19th Battalion
31 January 1916 - 31 January 1918

WO95/2490/5

The Naval & Military Press Ltd
www.nmarchive.com
Published in association with The National Archives

Published by

The Naval & Military Press Ltd

Unit 10 Ridgewood Industrial Park,

Uckfield, East Sussex,

TN22 5QE England

Tel: +44 (0) 1825 749494

www.naval-military-press.com

www.nmarchive.com

This diary has been reprinted in facsimile from the original. Any imperfections are inevitably reproduced and the quality may fall short of modern type and cartographic standards.

© **Crown Copyright**
Images reproduced by permission of The National Archives, London, England, 2015.

Contents

Document type	Place/Title	Date From	Date To
Heading	WO95/2490/5.		
Heading	35th Division 106th Infy Bde 19th Bn Durham Lt Infy Jan 1916-Jan 1918 To 104 Bde 35 Div.		
Heading	19th Durham L.I. Vol I 35th Feb 16-Feb 18.		
War Diary	Perham Down.	31/01/1916	31/01/1916
War Diary	Havre.	01/02/1916	03/02/1916
War Diary	St Omer.	04/02/1916	04/02/1916
War Diary	Campagne.	05/02/1916	08/02/1916
War Diary	Thiennes.	09/02/1916	09/02/1916
War Diary	Trenches.	10/02/1916	10/02/1916
War Diary	Thiennes.	11/02/1916	17/02/1916
War Diary	Les Lauriers.	18/02/1916	28/02/1916
War Diary	In The Trenches.	29/02/1916	29/02/1916
Miscellaneous	War Diary Appendix 1.		
Heading	19 D.L.I. Vol 2.		
War Diary	In The Trenches.	01/03/1916	01/03/1916
War Diary	Pont De Hem.	02/03/1916	03/03/1916
War Diary	In The Trenches.	04/03/1916	07/03/1916
War Diary	Pont De Hem.	08/03/1916	11/03/1916
War Diary	In The Trenches.	12/03/1916	15/03/1916
War Diary	La Gorgue.	16/03/1916	16/03/1916
War Diary	Les Lobes.	17/03/1916	19/03/1916
War Diary	Calonne	20/03/1916	26/03/1916
War Diary	Estaires.	27/03/1916	27/03/1916
War Diary	La Croix Lescornex.	28/03/1916	31/03/1916
War Diary	In The Trenches.	01/03/1916	01/03/1916
War Diary	Pont De Hem.	02/03/1916	03/03/1916
War Diary	In The Trenches.	04/03/1916	07/03/1916
War Diary	Pont De Hem.	08/03/1916	11/03/1916
War Diary	In The Trenches.	12/03/1916	15/03/1916
War Diary	La Corgue.	16/03/1916	16/03/1916
War Diary	Les Lobes.	17/03/1916	19/03/1916
War Diary	Calonne.	20/03/1916	26/03/1916
War Diary	Estaires.	27/03/1916	27/03/1916
War Diary	La Croix Lescornex.	28/03/1916	31/03/1916
War Diary	Appendix 1.	03/03/1916	03/03/1916
War Diary	Appendix 2.	11/03/1916	11/03/1916
War Diary	Appendix 3.	13/03/1916	13/03/1916
War Diary	Appendix 4.	14/03/1916	14/03/1916
War Diary	Appendix 5.	27/03/1916	27/03/1916
War Diary	Appendix. 6.	28/03/1916	28/03/1916
War Diary	Appendix. 1.	03/03/1916	03/03/1916
War Diary	Appendix. 2.	11/03/1916	11/03/1916
War Diary	Appendix. 3.	13/03/1916	13/03/1916
War Diary	Appendix 4.	14/03/1916	14/03/1916
War Diary	Appendix 5.	27/03/1916	27/03/1916
War Diary	Appendix 6.	28/03/1916	28/03/1916
War Diary	In The Trenches.	01/04/1916	04/04/1916
War Diary	Sailly.	05/04/1916	12/04/1916
War Diary	Laventie.	13/04/1916	15/04/1916

Type	Description	Date From	Date To
War Diary	Neuf Berquin.	16/04/1916	16/04/1916
War Diary	In The Trenches.	17/04/1916	20/04/1916
War Diary	Croix Barbee.	21/04/1916	24/04/1916
War Diary	In The Trenches.	25/04/1916	28/04/1916
War Diary	Vieille Chapelle.	29/04/1916	30/04/1916
War Diary	Appendix 1.	03/04/1916	03/04/1916
War Diary	Appendix. 2.	06/04/1916	06/04/1916
War Diary	Appendix 3.	06/04/1916	06/04/1916
War Diary	Appendix 4.	06/04/1916	06/04/1916
War Diary	Appendix 5.	12/04/1916	12/04/1916
War Diary	Appendix. 6.	14/04/1916	14/04/1916
War Diary	Appendix 7.	19/04/1916	19/04/1916
War Diary	Appendix 8.	29/04/1916	29/04/1916
War Diary	Appendix 9.	29/04/1916	29/04/1916
War Diary	Vieille Chapelle.	01/05/1916	06/05/1916
War Diary	Puhebourg St Vaast.	07/05/1916	10/05/1916
War Diary	In The Trenches.	11/05/1916	14/05/1916
War Diary	Richebourg St Vaast.	15/05/1916	18/05/1916
War Diary	In The Trenches.	19/05/1916	22/05/1916
War Diary	La Fosse.	23/05/1916	28/05/1916
War Diary	Le Touret.	29/05/1916	31/05/1916
War Diary	Appendix 1.	06/05/1916	06/05/1916
War Diary	Appendix 2.	08/05/1916	08/05/1916
War Diary	Appendix 3.	11/05/1916	11/05/1916
War Diary	Appendix 4.	17/05/1916	17/05/1916
War Diary	Appendix 5.	21/05/1916	21/05/1916
War Diary	Appendix 6.	23/05/1916	23/05/1916
War Diary	Appendix 7.	26/05/1916	26/05/1916
Miscellaneous	March Orders By Lieut. Colonel L.S. Stoney Commanding 19th (Service) Battalion The Durham Light Infantry.	04/05/1916	04/05/1916
Miscellaneous	Move Orders By Major E.L. Maxwell Tempy. Commdg 19th (Service) Battalion The Durham Light Infantry.	10/05/1916	10/05/1916
Miscellaneous	Move Orders By Major E.L. Maxwell Tempy. Commanding 19th (Service) Battalion. The Durham Light Infantry.	13/05/1916	13/05/1916
Miscellaneous	Move Orders By Major E.L. Maxwell Tempy Commanding 19th (Service) Battalion The Durham Light Infantry. No., 1.	17/05/1916	17/05/1916
Miscellaneous	Move Orders By Major E.L. Maxwell Tempy Commanding 19th (Service) Battalion The Durham Light Infantry. No., 2.	20/05/1916	20/05/1916
Miscellaneous	19th (S) Battalion The Durham Light Infantry.	28/05/1916	28/05/1916
War Diary	Le Touret.	01/06/1916	01/06/1916
War Diary	In The Trenches.	02/06/1916	05/06/1916
War Diary	Le Touret.	06/06/1916	10/06/1916
War Diary	Fosse.	11/06/1916	15/06/1916
War Diary	Gonnehem.	16/06/1916	30/06/1916
War Diary	Appendix. 1	02/06/1916	02/06/1916
War Diary	Appendix 2.	06/06/1916	06/06/1916
War Diary	Appendix 3	11/06/1916	11/06/1916
War Diary	Appendix 4	22/06/1916	22/06/1916
War Diary	Appendix 5	23/06/1916	23/06/1916
War Diary	Appendix 6	25/06/1916	25/06/1916

Heading	106th Bde. 35th Div. War Diary 19th Battalion Durham Light Infantry 1st to 31st July 1916. Report on Operations 29/30th July with G.S. Diary.			
War Diary	Gonnehem.		01/07/1916	03/07/1916
War Diary	Le Souich.		04/07/1916	31/07/1916
War Diary	Appendix 1.		15/07/1916	15/07/1916
War Diary	Appendix 2.		17/07/1916	17/07/1916
War Diary	Appendix 3.		18/07/1916	18/07/1916
War Diary	Appendix 4.		19/07/1916	19/07/1916
War Diary	Appendix 5.		22/05/1916	22/05/1916
War Diary	Appendix 7.		25/07/1916	25/07/1916
War Diary	Appendix 6.		24/07/1916	24/07/1916
War Diary	Appendix 8.		27/07/1916	27/07/1916
War Diary	Appendix 9.		28/07/1916	28/07/1916
Heading	106th Infantry Brigade. 35th Division. 1/19th Battalion Durham Light Infantry August 1916.			
War Diary			01/08/1916	31/08/1916
War Diary	Appendix. 1.		05/08/1916	05/08/1916
War Diary	Appendix. 2.		16/08/1916	16/08/1916
War Diary	Appendix 3		17/08/1916	17/08/1916
War Diary	Appendix 4		27/08/1916	27/08/1916
War Diary	Appendix 5		31/08/1916	31/08/1916
War Diary			01/09/1916	31/10/1916
War Diary	Appendix 1.		02/10/1916	02/10/1916
War Diary	Appendix 2.		11/10/1916	11/10/1916
War Diary	Appendix 3.		19/10/1916	19/10/1916
War Diary	Appendix 4.		19/10/1916	19/10/1916
War Diary			01/11/1916	30/11/1916
War Diary	Appendix 1.		01/11/1916	01/11/1916
War Diary	Appendix 2.		08/11/1916	08/11/1916
War Diary	Appendix 3.		09/11/1916	09/11/1916
War Diary	Appendix 4.		17/11/1916	17/11/1916
War Diary	Appendix 5.		26/11/1916	26/11/1916
War Diary	Appendix 6.		27/11/1916	27/11/1916
War Diary	Appendix 7.		29/11/1916	29/11/1916
War Diary			01/12/1916	31/01/1917
War Diary	Appendix 1.		09/01/1917	09/01/1917
War Diary	Appendix 2.		10/01/1917	10/01/1917
War Diary	Appendix 3.		12/01/1917	12/01/1917
War Diary	Appendix 4.		14/01/1917	14/01/1917
War Diary	Appendix 5.		15/01/1917	15/01/1917
War Diary	Appendix 6.		16/01/1917	16/01/1917
War Diary	Appendix 7.		21/01/1917	21/01/1917
War Diary	Appendix 8.		23/01/1917	23/01/1917
War Diary			01/02/1917	28/02/1917
War Diary	Appendix 1.		05/02/1917	05/02/1917
War Diary	Appendix 2.		07/02/1917	07/02/1917
War Diary	Appendix 3.		09/02/1917	09/02/1917
War Diary	Appendix 4.		13/02/1917	13/02/1917
War Diary	Appendix 5.		14/02/1917	14/02/1917
War Diary	Appendix 6.		21/02/1917	21/02/1917
War Diary	Appendix 7.		23/02/1917	23/02/1917
War Diary			01/03/1917	31/03/1917
War Diary	Appendix 1.		01/03/1917	01/03/1917
War Diary	Appendix 2		02/03/1917	02/03/1917
War Diary	Appendix 3		05/03/1917	05/03/1917

Type	Description	Start	End
War Diary	Appendix 4	07/03/1917	07/03/1917
War Diary	Appendix 5	10/03/1917	10/03/1917
War Diary	Appendix 6	11/03/1917	11/03/1917
War Diary	Appendix 7	16/03/1917	16/03/1917
War Diary	Appendix 8	21/03/1917	21/03/1917
War Diary	Appendix 9	30/03/1917	30/03/1917
War Diary		01/04/1917	30/04/1917
War Diary	Appendix 1.	02/04/1917	02/04/1917
War Diary	Appendix 2	03/04/1917	03/04/1917
War Diary	Appendix 3	13/04/1917	13/04/1917
War Diary	Appendix 4	15/04/1917	15/04/1917
War Diary	Appendix 5	16/04/1917	16/04/1917
War Diary	Appendix 6	18/04/1917	18/04/1917
War Diary	Appendix 7	21/02/1917	21/02/1917
War Diary	Appendix 8	22/04/1917	22/04/1917
War Diary	Appendix 9	24/04/1917	24/04/1917
War Diary	Appendix 10	29/04/1917	29/04/1917
War Diary		01/05/1917	31/05/1917
War Diary	Appendix 1	01/05/1917	01/05/1917
War Diary	Appendix 2	05/05/1917	06/05/1917
War Diary	Appendix 3	12/05/1917	12/05/1917
War Diary	Appendix 4	28/05/1917	28/05/1917
War Diary		01/06/1917	30/06/1917
War Diary	Appendix 1	03/06/1917	03/06/1917
War Diary	Appendix 2	06/06/1917	06/06/1917
War Diary	Appendix 3	12/06/1917	12/06/1917
War Diary	Appendix 4	22/06/1917	22/06/1917
Miscellaneous	Officer Commanding, 17th R. Scots.	11/06/1917	11/06/1917
War Diary		01/07/1917	31/07/1917
War Diary	Appendix 1	01/07/1917	01/07/1917
War Diary	Appendix 2	05/07/1917	05/07/1917
War Diary	Appendix 3	10/07/1917	10/07/1917
War Diary	Appendix 4	12/07/1917	12/07/1917
War Diary	Appendix 5	13/07/1917	13/07/1917
War Diary	Appendix 6	14/07/1917	14/07/1917
War Diary	Appendix 7	23/07/1917	23/07/1917
War Diary	Appendix 8	27/07/1917	27/07/1917
War Diary	Appendix 9	31/07/1917	31/07/1917
War Diary		01/08/1917	31/08/1917
Miscellaneous	19 Bn Durham L.I. Appendix to War Diary.	03/09/1917	03/09/1917
Operation(al) Order(s)	Operation Order No. 95.		
War Diary		01/09/1917	30/09/1917
War Diary	Appendix 1	06/09/1917	06/09/1917
War Diary	Appendix 2	10/09/1917	10/09/1917
War Diary	Appendix 3	11/09/1917	11/09/1917
War Diary	Appendix 4	14/09/1917	14/09/1917
War Diary	Appendix 5	24/09/1917	24/09/1917
War Diary	Appendix 6	29/09/1917	29/09/1917
War Diary	Appendix 7	29/09/1917	29/09/1917
War Diary		01/10/1917	31/10/1917
War Diary	Appendix 1	08/10/1917	08/10/1917
War Diary	Appendix 2.	15/10/1917	15/10/1917
War Diary	Appendix 4	29/10/1917	29/10/1917
War Diary	Appendix 5	31/10/1917	31/10/1917
War Diary		01/11/1917	30/11/1917
War Diary	Appendix 1.	11/12/1916	11/12/1916

War Diary	Appendix 2.	18/12/1916	18/12/1916
War Diary	Appendix 3.	24/12/1916	24/12/1916
War Diary	Appendix 4.	26/12/1916	26/12/1916
War Diary	Appendix 5.	31/12/1916	31/12/1916
Miscellaneous	Appendix VI.	04/12/1917	04/12/1917
War Diary	Appendix 5	19/11/1917	20/11/1917
War Diary	Appendix 6	19/11/1917	19/11/1917
War Diary	Appendix 7	21/11/1917	21/11/1917
War Diary	Appendix 8	22/11/1917	22/11/1917
War Diary	Appendix 9	25/11/1917	25/11/1917
War Diary	Appendix 10		
War Diary		01/12/1917	31/12/1917
War Diary	Appendix 1.	01/11/1917	01/11/1917
War Diary	Appendix 2	01/11/1917	04/11/1917
War Diary	Appendix 3	08/11/1917	08/11/1917
War Diary	Appendix 4	09/11/1917	09/11/1917
War Diary		01/01/1918	31/01/1918

W0a5/2490/5

35TH DIVISION
106TH INFY BDE

19TH BN DURHAM LT INFY

JAN ~~FEB~~ 1916 - JAN ~~FEB~~ 1918

~~FROM~~

TO 104 BDE 35 DIV

19th Durham L.I.
Vol I 35½

Feb '16
1
Feb '18

WAR DIARY
or
INTELLIGENCE SUMMARY.
(Erase heading not required.)

Army Form C. 2118

Instructions regarding War Diaries and Intelligence Summaries are contained in F.S. Regs., Part II. and the Staff Manual respectively. Title Pages will be prepared in manuscript.

Place	Date	Hour	Summary of Events and Information	Remarks and references to Appendices
PERHAM DOWN	Jan 31st	3 a.m.	Left PERHAM DOWN for SOUTHAMPTON	
HAVRE	Feb 1st		HAVRE. No 1 Rest Camp SANVIC.	
HAVRE	Feb 2nd		HAVRE:	
HAVRE	Feb 3rd	2.30 pm	Left HAVRE 2.30 pm.	
SEOMER	Feb 4th	12 noon	arrived SEOMER 12 noon.	
CAMPAGNE	Feb 5th		in billets CAMPAGNE. 4 mls S.E of SEOMER.	
CAMPAGNE	Feb 6th		in billets CAMPAGNE.	
CAMPAGNE	Feb 7th		in billets CAMPAGNE.	
CAMPAGNE	Feb 8th		in billets CAMPAGNE. Four officers & P.N.C.O.'s sent to Canads Division	Pt Offrs dis 1.
THIENNES	Feb 9th		in billets here. Inspected by Sir Douglas Haig & Prince Arthur of Connaught. THIENNES 31 miles E of AIRE. Officer to Canads detailed noted SEVENANT	9 Offrs dis 2
THIENNES	Feb 10th		in billets here. Canadian Descents arrested & handed over to Provost Marshall.	
THIENNES	Feb 11th		in billets. Inspected by LORD KITCHENER	12 offrs dis 3.
THIENNES	Feb 12th		in billets. 1 officer & 30 men sent to R.E. Parc.	
THIENNES	Feb 13th		in billets.	
THIENNES	Feb 14th		in billets. Four officers & D.N.C.O. return from Canads Division.	
THIENNES	Feb 15th		in billets.	
THIENNES	Feb 16th		in billets.	
THIENNES	Feb 17th		in billets.	
LES LAURIERS	Feb 18th		marched to billets here.	
LES LAURIERS	Feb 19th		in billets.	
LES LAURIERS	Feb 20th		in billets.	
LES LAURIERS	Feb 21st		in billets.	
LES LAURIERS	Feb 22nd		in billets.	
LES LAURIERS	Feb 23rd		in billets.	
LES LAURIERS	Feb 24th		in billets.	
LES LAURIERS	Feb 25th		in billets.	
LES LAURIERS	Feb 26th		in billets.	
LES LAURIERS	Feb 27th		in billets. Now ordered off to trenches to be attached to 57th Brigade.	
LES LAURIERS	Feb 28th	10.45 am	attached to 57th Brigade.	
the Trenches	Feb 29th			

WAR DIARY

Appendix 1

8th Feb. Following attached to Guards Division in trenches for instruction.

    W coy   Major OSLER
    X coy   Capt KINCH
    Y coy   Capt WARMINGTON
    Z coy   Capt CAMERON.

    W coy   Sgt GREEN & Sgt WHITE.
    X coy   Sgt ROGERSON & Sgt ARMSTRONG.
    Y coy   Sgt JOHNSON & Cpl THORLEY.
    Z coy   Sgt WRIGHTSON & Sgt THOMAS.

The above returned to the batt on 15th inst.

Appendix 2.

9th Feb. 2/Lt CARROLL attached to trench mortar school at ST VENANT and returned to batt 20th inst.

Appendix 3.

12th Feb. 2/Lt RYALL and 50 men of No 7 Platoon X coy attached for duty with FOREST CONTROL CENTRE LE PARC. Forest of NIEPPE.

                                R.H. Hodgson
                                     Lt & Adjt
                                     19th Durh. L.I.

1771 Vol 2

WAR DIARY
or
INTELLIGENCE SUMMARY

Army Form C. 2118

(Erase heading not required.)

Instructions regarding War Diaries and Intelligence Summaries are contained in F. S. Regs., Part II. and the Staff Manual respectively. Title Pages will be prepared in manuscript.

35th Divn 7. 19th (S) Batt Durh. L.I. for March 1916.

WAR OFFICE RECEIVED -4 APR 1916

Place	Date 1916	Hour	Summary of Events and Information	Remarks and references to Appendices
The trenches	1st March		Attached to 57th BDE at PONT DE HEM	
PONT DE HEM	2nd "		in billets	
PONT DE HEM	3rd "	6:30 p.m.	Batt. attached to 57th Bde and went into trenches this evening with reserve units of 57 Bde.	1.
The trenches	4th March		in the trenches, weather fair. Casualties Nil.	
"	5th "		" " weather changed, rather cold. Some snow. Casualties Nil.	
"	6th "		in the trenches	
"	7th "	7 p.m.	in the trenches. weather improved, but raining. Casualties Nil.	
PONT DE HEM	8th "		in billets, whole batt relieved from trench at 7 p.m.	
PONT DE HEM	9th "		in billets	
PONT DE HEM	10th "		in billets, whole batt. relieved with reserve units of that Bde. but in same billeting area.	
PONT DE HEM	11th "		in billets	
The trenches	12th "		Batt into trenches, weather practically no wind. Casualties Nil.	
The trenches	13th "	11:20 am	in trenches. 2nd in command left for India. Evening showed a certain amount of artillery activity about noon, 2 men wounded.	2.
The trenches	14th "	10:50am	Batt in trenches. Enemy having effected a mine in front of trench on our right, pushed to sell our front line heavily with H.E + Trgs + Gas shells	3.
The trenches	15th "	7:20 p.m.	Batt – no further casualties. Weather fair. Raining gently. Still 4 more of our shells of previous day, lodging about trenches. Batt relieved by 10th Batt WORCESTERS that night A went to billets at LA GORGUE for the night	4.
LA GORGUE	16th "	10 am	Batt. Left LA GORGUE for LES LOBES in the morning.	
LES LOBES	17th "		Batt. in billets, near LOCON	
LES LOBES	18th "		Batt. in billets	
LES LOBES	19th "	10:15 am	Batt. in billets, but left for CALONNE in the morning for new billets.	
CALONNE	20th "		Batt in billets	
CALONNE	21st "		Batt in billets	
CALONNE	22nd "		Batt in billets	
CALONNE	23rd "		Batt in billets	
CALONNE	24th "		Batt in billets	
CALONNE	25th "		Batt in billets	
CALONNE	26th "		Batt in billets	
ESTAIRES	27th "	11 am	Batt in billets, left at 2 p.m. in Brigade for ESTAIRES for that night	5.
LA CROIX LES CORNET	28th "		Batt in billets, left early in the morning and marched by Companies to LA CROIX LES CORNET.	6.
LA CROIX LES CORNET	29th "		Batt in billets. Weather fine, high Easterly wind.	
LA CROIX LES CORNET	30th "		Batt in billets	
LA CROIX LES CORNET	31st "	7:15 p.m.	Batt in billets, but relieved 17th Batt W. YORK Regt in the trenches this evening. Weather fine. Casualties Nil.	

Army Form C. 2118

WAR DIARY
of 19th (S) batt Durh. L.I.
INTELLIGENCE SUMMARY for March 1916.
(Erase heading not required.)

Instructions regarding War Diaries and Intelligence Summaries are contained in F. S. Regs., Part II. and the Staff Manual respectively. Title Pages will be prepared in manuscript.

Place	Date 1916	Hour	Summary of Events and Information	Remarks and references to Appendices
In the trenches	1st March		Attached to 57th Bde	
PONT DE HEM	2nd "		1 killed	1.
PONT DE HEM	3rd "	6.30 pm	Batt. attached to 57th Bde and went into trenches this evening with reserve coy of Pont Bde.	
In the trenches	4th March		1 killed	
In the trenches	5th "		1 killed — weather colder, rather cold, snow shower. Casualties Nil.	
In the trenches	6th "		1 killed	
PONT DE HEM	7th "	7 pm	1 killed	
PONT DE HEM	8th "		Batt. on relief, marched out to Pont de Hem, where batt. will remain till relieved from trenches 2pm	
PONT DE HEM	9th "		1 killed	Casualties Nil.
PONT DE HEM	10th "		1 killed — weather broken, wind of Pont Bde, but have billeting area.	
PONT DE HEM	11th "		1 killed — weather broken, windier, warmer. Yesterday no wind. Casualties Nil.	
In the trenches	12th "			
In the trenches	13th "		Batt — in trenches	
In the trenches	14th "	11.20 am	Batt in trenches 2nd in command left for India. Enemy showed a certain amount of artillery activity about noon. 2 men wounded.	2.
In the trenches	15th "	10.55 am	Batt in the trenches. Fine, hazy morning. Also planted a mine in front of batt. on our right. Batt. to will as part but trench to will will with H.E. & Shrap. (Gas shells 3.	
In the trenches	16th "	7.20 pm	Batt in relief trenches. Canadian Batt. relieved 2/10.5 batt WORCESTERS 7.20pm pt, 3 men killed & 3 wounded. Casualties 4	4.
LA GORGUE	16th "	10 am	Batt — killed. Batt to GORGUE for LES LOBES in morning.	
LES LOBES	17th "		Batt — killed, near LOCON	
LES LOBES	18th "		Batt — killed	
LES LOBES	19th "	10.15 am	Batt — killed, Batt left for CALONNE in morning for new billets	
CALONNE	20th "		Batt — killed	
CALONNE	21st "		Batt — killed	
CALONNE	22nd "		Batt — killed	
CALONNE	23rd "		Batt — killed	
CALONNE	24th "		Batt — killed	
CALONNE	25th "		Batt — killed	
CALONNE	26th "		Batt — killed	
ESTAIRES	27th "	9 am	Batt — killed, left at 9am in brigade for ESTAIRES for that night and repl marched by Companies to LA CROIX LES CORNET	5.
LA CROIX LES CORNET	28th "		Batt — killed. Weather fine, high winds, warm.	
LA CROIX LES CORNET	29th "		Batt — killed	6.
LA CROIX LES CORNET	30th "		Batt — killed	
LA CROIX LES CORNET	31st "	7.15 pm	Batt — killed, Batt relieved 17th batt W. YORK Reg't in the trenches this evening. Weather fine. Casualties Nil.	

WAR DIARY.

Appendix 1.
3rd March.

Batt attached to 57th Bde as followes.

Comdg Officer
Adjt } To 10th batt Warwickshire Regt.
"X" coy 19th D.L.I. " " " "

2nd in Command
M.G. Officer } To 8th batt Gloucester Regt.
"W" coy 19th D.L.I. " " " "

M.O.
Signalling Officer } To 10th batt Worcester Regt.
"Y" coy 19th D.L.I. " " " "

Q.M.
"Z" coy 19th D.L.I. } To 8th batt N. Staffordshire Regt.

Appendix 2.
11th March.

Batt went into the trenches as a complete unit, and no longer attached 57 Bde. But we are still attached to 19th DIVISION. We relieved 17th W. Yorks at 7.30 pm.

Appendix 3.
13th March.

Major E.L. Maxwell, 2nd in Command, recalled to Indian Army; authority G.H.Q letter dated 8/3/16 No A/9547.

Appendix 4.
14th March.

Enemy shelled our front line pretty heavily in the morning. But only 17 casualties in batt. 1 man later died of wounds.

Appendix 5.
27th March.

Relieved 2nd Batt Royal Berkshire regiment, in support billets. The 35th Div having taken over a new line from 8th Div.

Appendix 6.
28th March.

A draft arrived this day from the base, consisting of 3 N.C.O's & 68 men.

R.J. Hodgson
Lt & Adjt.

WAR DIARY.

Appendix 1.
3rd March

Batt attached to 57th Bde as follows:-
Commdg Officer   }
Adjt   } to 10th Batt Warwickshire Regt
"X" coy 19th D.L.I.

2nd in Command   }
M.G. Officer   } to 8th Batt Gloucester Regt
"W" coy 19th D.L.I.

M.O.   }
Signalling Officer} to 10th Batt Worcester Regt
"Y" coy 19th D.L.I.

Q.M.   }
                  } to 8th Batt N. Staffordshire Regt.
"Z" coy 19th D.L.I.

Appendix 2.
11th March

Batt went into the trenches as a complete unit, and no longer attached 57 Bde. But we are still attached to 19th DIVISION. We relieved 17th W. Yorks at 7.30 pm.

Appendix 3.
13th March

Major E.L. Maxwell, 2nd in Command, recalled to Indian Army; authority G.H.Q. letter dated 8/3/16 No A/9547.

Appendix 4.
14th March

Enemy shelled our front line pretty heavily in the morning. But only 1 casualty in batt. 1 man killed died of wounds.

Appendix 5.
27th March

Relieved 1st Batt Royal Berkshire regiment in support billets. The 35th Div having taken over a new line from 8th Div.

Appendix 6.
28th March

A draft arrived this day from the base, consisting of 3 N.C.O's & 68 men.

R.F. Hodgson
Lt & Adjt.

XXXV 17 D.L.I.

Army Form C. 2118

of 19F(S) Batt. Durh. L.I.
Vol. 3
for April 1916.

WAR DIARY
INTELLIGENCE SUMMARY
(Erase heading not required.)

Instructions regarding War Diaries and Intelligence Summaries are contained in F.S. Regs., Part II. and the Staff Manual respectively. Title Pages will be prepared in manuscript.

Place	Date 1916	Hour	Summary of Events and Information	Remarks and references to Appendices
In the Trenches	1st April		Weather fine day and night, quiet and uneventful. Casualties Nil	
In the Trenches	2nd "		Sgt M Dutch died, day uneventful. One man killed & 2 slightly wounded	
In the Trenches	3rd "		No wind. Fine weather continues. One man killed in front line.	
In the Trenches	4th "	8.25pm	Day uneventful. Casualties Nil. Enemy very quiet, 1 officer & 32 other ranks to course at Pont Borle officers due 3rd	
SAILLY	5th April		Batt. relieved by 23rd Battn MANCHESTER Regt, at 9.25 pm. Batt. marched to billets at SAILLY	
SAILLY	6th "		Draft of one man received from hospital. rest of from base.	
SAILLY	7th "		Batt. in billets. 1 officer & 5 men on course at Pont French motor school. 1 officer & men on course Div T.M. School. 3 officers & 3 N.C.Os Field Engineer Course	2. 3. 4.
SAILLY	8th "		Batt. in billets	
SAILLY	9th "		Batt. in billets	
SAILLY	10th "		Batt. in billets	
SAILLY	11th "		Batt. in billets. Major F.L. MAXWELL assumed the Batt. for duty, as 2nd in Command.	
SAILLY	12th "		Batt. in billets	
SAILLY	13th "	9.15 pm	Batt. in billets. 3 men out on Vickers gun Course. Batt. relieved 15th Batt CHESHIRE Regt in "Support billets" LAVENTIE.	5.
LAVENTIE	14th "		Batt. in billets. 2 men out on Special Sniping Course.	
LAVENTIE	15th "	9.10 pm	Batt. relieved by 11th Battn SOUTH WALES BORDERERS & then moved to billets at NEUF BERQUIN	6.
NEUF BERQUIN	16th April	12.30 pm	Batt. relieved 7th Battn LOYAL NORTH LANCASHIRE Regt in NEUVE CHAPELLE Reserve section. Relief complete by 9.15 pm	
In the Trenches	17th "		Weather fine. Wind in West. Fresh strong. 2 men killed. 2/Lt FARKINER attached to 106/1 T.M. batt.	
In the Trenches	18th "		Weather & other conditions good. 1 man wounded. 2/Lt COFFEY attached to 255 Trenches Coy.	7.
In the Trenches	19th "		Wind still in west. fairly steady breeze. Casualties Nil.	
In the Trenches	20th "	9.20 pm	Batt. relieved by 17th Battn W. YORK Regt, and marched to 2nd Poste Bombing School. 4 N.C.O's & 12 men to supp't billets at CROIX BARBEE. 1 man wounded.	
CROIX BARBEE	21st April		Batt. in Support billets. Day quiet and uneventful.	
CROIX BARBEE	22nd "		Batt. in Support billets.	
CROIX BARBEE	23rd "	10 noon	Batt. in Support billets. Enemy shelled near H.A. billets in morning. No damage done & One man wounded.	
CROIX BARBEE	24th "	9.20 pm	Batt. in Support billets. Batt. relieved 17th Batt in YORKSHIRE Regt in trenches without incident	
In the Trenches	25th "		Weather windy & warm. No casualties.	
In the Trenches	26th "		No wind at all. Fine weather continues.	
In the Trenches	27th "		Weather hot. Enemy shell reserve line & Communication trench. 4 men wounded. Capt. E. CAMERON Admitted Hospital dysentery (Auth XI (Cop C 206/38)	
In the Trenches	28th "	10 pm day	Batt. in billets. 3 officers + 5 N.C.O. to Div School of Field Engineering.	
VIEILLE CHAPELLE	29th "			
VIEILLE CHAPELLE	30th April		Day uneventful. Sgt Ladnig was killed. Batt. relieved by 17th Batt LANCASHIRE FUSILIERS, & moved in Reserve billets at VIEILLE CHAPELLE. 1 officer. 32 other ranks to Brade Bombing school.	8. 9.

WAR DIARY.

Appendix 1.
3rd April 1916.
Bde Bombing School formed at ROUGE de BOUT. 1st Course commenced 3rd inst. 2/Lt R. CROSS and 8 men from each Company attended. Course finished on 13th inst.

Appendix 2.
6th April.
Lieut W.J. Oliver and 5 men from "Z" Company attended a five day Course at Bde Trench Mortar School.

Appendix 3.
6th April.
Lieut C.B. Pearson and 6 men attend a weeks course of instruction at Div Trench Mortar School.

Appendix 4.
6th April.
2/Lieut W.V. FALKINER.
2/Lieut J.W. RYALL.
and 2/Lieut R.C. MACLACHLAN
with 3 N.C.O's attend a Course of instruction at DIV School of FIELD ENGINEERING in NOUVEAU MONDE, for 6 days.

Appendix 5.
12th April.
3 men detailed for Course of instruction in VICKERS machine gun work under O.C. No 6 Motor M.G. Battery near SAILLY.

Appendix 6.
14th April.
2 men of Y Company sent on special Sniping Course at STEENBECQUE for one week.

Appendix 7.
19th April.
4 N.C.O's (one per Company) and 3 men per company sent to 2nd Course at Bde Bombing School.

Appendix 8.
29th April.
Capt T. KINCH.
Lieut. C.B. PEARSON
and 2/Lieut F. MOORE
with 3 N.C.O's attend 3rd Course of Field Engineering at Div School of Engineering at CHATEAU for one week.

Appendix 9.
29th April.
2/Lieut A.S. CARROLL
with 1 N.C.O & 7 men per Company to Bde Bombing School at PACAUT for Course of Instruction.

25/16 XXXV Vol 4

WAR DIARY ~~or~~ **INTELLIGENCE SUMMARY**
(Erase heading not required.)

Army Form C. 2118

of 19th (S) Battalion
The Durham Light Infantry
for month of MAY 1916.

Instructions regarding War Diaries and Intelligence Summaries are contained in F. S. Regs., Part II. and the Staff Manual respectively. Title Pages will be prepared in manuscript.

Place	Date	Hour	Summary of Events and Information	Remarks and references to Appendices
VIEILLE CHAPELLE	May 1		Battn. in billets	
"	2		-do-	
"	3		-do-	
"	4		-do-	
"	5		-do-	
"	6		Battn. in billets	
RICHEBOURG ST VAAST	7		Battn. moved to Richebourg St Vaast at 1 p.m. in Brigade Reserve & took over billets from 15th Cheshire Regt.	
"	8			
"	9			
"	10			
In the Trenches	11		Battn. moved at 9.0 p.m. & took over trenches from 17th West Yorkshire Regt. in left sub-sector FERME du BOIS Section. Relief completed without incident. Situation normal	
"	12		-do-	
"	13		-do-	
RICHEBOURG ST VAAST	14		Battn. relieved in the trenches by 17th West Yorkshire Regt. and relief completed without incident.	
"	15		Battn. in billets	
"	16		-do-	
"	17		-do-	
"	18		-do-	
In the Trenches	19		Battn. moved at 9.0 p.m. and relieved 17th West Yorkshire Regt. in the left sub-sector FERME du BOIS Section. Relief completed without incident.	
"	20		-do-	
"	21		-do-	
LA FOSSE	22		Battn. relieved by 17th Lancashire Fusiliers without incident & moved into Divisional rest at LA FOSSE	
"	23		Battn. in billets	
"	24		-do-	
"	25		-do-	
"	26		-do-	
"	27		-do-	
"	28		At 4-10 p.m. received orders from 106th Brigade to "stand to" & be ready to move at short notice. Received orders from 106th Brigade to move. Battn. moved to LE TOURET and there took over billets from Northamptonshire Regt.	
DE TOURET	29		Battn. in billets	
"	30		-do-	
"	31		-do- orders rec'd from 106th Brigade at 8-30 p.m. to "stand to" in case of hostile attack on left front. Heavy bombardment on our left.	

WAR DIARY.

Appendix 1.
6th May 1916.
Lieut. R.E.Hodgson returned for duty to his Regiment 1st North Staffordshires.

Appendix 2.
8th May 1916.
Lieut.Colonel L.S.Stoney proceeded on leave to England and Major E.L.Maxwell took over command of the Battalion during his absence.

Appendix 3.
11th May 1916.
2nd Lieut W.F.Reeve reported for duty on first appointment and was posted to 'W' Company.

Appendix 4.
17th May 1916.
A Draft of 8 men arrived from the Base and were taken on the strength of the Battalion.

Appendix 5.
21st May 1916.
40 other ranks arrived from Base and were taken on the strength of the Battalion.

Appendix 6.
23rd May 1916.
Lieut Colonel, L.S.Stoney having returned from leave assumed command of the Battalion.

Appendix 7.
26th May 1916.
Lieut J.Phillips reported for duty as Transport Officer on first appointment.
Major E.L.Maxwell left the Battalion to take over Command of 23rd Manchester Regiment, 104th Infantry Brigade, vice Lieut.Colonel Smith.

E. Jameson, Capt.
Adjutant.
19th (S.) Bn. Durham Light Infantry.

S E C R E T.   ~~MARCH~~ ORDERS BY

LIEUT.COLONEL L.S.STONEY COMMANDING

19th (SERVICE) BATTALION THE DURHAM LIGHT INFANTRY: 4-5-16.

1. The Battalion will relieve the 15th Cheshire Regiment at RICHEBOURG ST VAAST. on the 6th inst.

2. Lists of maps, trench stores etc., taken over will be rendered to Orderly Room by 10 a.m. 7th MAY.

3. All movements will be by sections.

4. Brigade Headquarters will close at VIEILLE CHAPELLE at 3pm and will reopen same hour at CENSE de RAUX. (Q.28.a.8.9).

5. The following posts will be found by 'Y' Company.

Post.	Garrison.	Map reading.
DOGS.	½ platoon.	S.9.b.2½.8½.
EDWARD.	½ "	S.9.a.9.8
HENS	½ "	S.3.d.1.3.
RICHEBOURG	1 "	S.2.c.3.1
HUNTER	4 men	S.8.a.2.3
SCOTT.	4 men	S.8.a.2.0.

   "X" Coy will find the following posts
   Grotto)
   Angle)   ½ platoon   S.2.a.8.8

6. Officers Commanding 'Y' and 'X' Coys will arrange to have all these posts relieved and properly taken over by 2pm on the 6th. They will report at RICHEBOURG Battn H.Q at 1 p.m. where guides will meet them.

7. Signalling Officer will relieve by 2 p.m.

8. The Battalion will parade at 1 p.m. and proceed to RICHEBOURG in the following order
   "W" Coy: "X" Coy "Z" Coy
   remainder of 'Y' Coy and Headquarters Coy.
   Guides will meet them at S.1.d.9.9

9. Transport Officer will arrange for the necessary transport, details of which will be issued later.

10. ROUTE-   VIEILLE CHAPELLE R.28.d.5.5. - RICHEBOURG.

CAPT & ADJUTANT.
19th (S) BN THE DURHAM LIGHT I.

S_E_C_R_E_T.   MOVE ORDERS BY

MAJOR E.L.MAXWELL TEMPY. COMMDG

19th (SERVICE) BATTALION THE DURHAM LIGHT INFANTRY.

10th May 1916.

1. The Battalion will take over trenches tonight from 17th (S) Bn West Yorkshire Regiment.

2. Companies will relieve in the following order, viz:-

   Left 'Z' Company.
   Right 'X' "
   Centre 'W' "
   Reserve 'Y' "
   H.Q.Coy.

   and will be met by guides at WHISKEY CORNER, "Z" Coy leading at 8.40 p.m, with 3 minutes interval between rear of one Company and head of next.

3. Parties for posts will march in rear of their companies.

   ## POSTS AND RESERVE COMPANY.

4. 'X' Company will have 1 platoon and 1 Lewis Gun PALL MALL KEEP.
   'W'   "   "   "   1   "   " 1 Vickers Gun FACTORY KEEP.
   'Z'   "   "   "   1   "   " 1 Lewis Gun LEFT GUARDS
   'Y'   "   "   "   2   "   BUTE ST.
   'Y'   "   "   "   2   " (less 15 men) RIGHT GUARDS.
   'Y'   "   "   " 15 men and 1 Vickers Gun COPSE KEEP.

5. All movements will be by sections at 200 yards interval.

                                              Capt & Adjt.
                                       19th (S) Bn The Durham Light I

S E C R E T.

MOVE ORDERS BY

MAJOR R.L.MAXWELL TEMPY COMMANDING

19th (SERVICE) BATTALION.THE DURHAM LIGHT INFANTRY

13th May 1916.

1. The Battalion will be relieved by 17th (S)Bn West Yorkshire Regt. on night of 14th instant and will go into same billets at RICHEBURG ST VAAST.

2. All movements to billets will be by sections.

3. Battalion specialists will be relieved as follows:-
   Snipers   9 a.m.
   Signallers   10.30 a.m.
   Lewis Guns.   12 noon.

4. The 17th (S) Bn West Yorkshire Regt will reach WHISKEY CORNER by 8.45 p.m. and will relieve as follows,viz:-
   1. Left Coy 'A'. 19th D.L.I.
   2. Right " 'C'   -do-
   3. Centre " 'B'   -do-
   4. Reserve" 'Y'   -do-
   5. Headquarters. Company.

5. Left Company will not move down Copse Street until relief of Centre Company is complete.

6. Baggage will reach Bute Street Dump not later than 8.0p.m. and be pushed down to Ration dump where Transport Officer will arrange to have the necessary transport waiting for it.

7. Lieut J.Bundy will arrange to be at Richebourg by 2 p.m. to take over billets etc., and Second Lt F.Moore will accompany him for instruction.

8. Angle and Grotto Posts will again be taken over by 'Y' Company but Scott and Hunters Posts will be permanently occupied by 17th (S) Bn West Yorkshire Regiment.

                                            E. Cameron
                                            Capt & Adjt.
                                      19th (S) Bn The Durham Light In.

SECRET.

MOVE ORDERS BY No.,____

MAJOR E.L. MAXWELL TEMPY COMMANDING

19th (SERVICE) BATTALION THE DURHAM LIGHT INFANTRY.

No., 1.   17th May 1916.

1. The 19th Durham Light Infantry will relieve 17th W.Yorks Regt in left subsector, Ferme du Bois Section on May 18th. There will be no guides.

2. Snipers will relieve by 9 a.m.
   Signallers "   "   " 10.30 a.m.
   Lewis Gunners &
   Bombers will relieve by 12 noon.
   All movements by day will be in parties of not more than 6 at 200 yards interval. By Night companies will move by Sections in file, at 200 yards interval with 3 minutes between companies.

3. 1 Officer per Company and 1 N.C.O. Per platoon will go into the line before 6 p.m. Lists of stores taken over will be forwarded to the Adjutant the same night.

4. Companies will hold the same frontage and posts as before Order of relief:- LEFT, RIGHT, CENTRE, RESERVE.
   'Z' Company will march off at 8.40 p.m.
   'X'   "   "   wHen 'Z' Company is clear.
   'W'   "   "   "   'X'   "   "   "   "
   'Y'   "   "   "   'W'   "   "   "   "
   Officers Commanding 'Y' and 'X' Companies will leave 2 men in each post until relieved by 17th West Yorks Regt. These men will then rejoin their companies.

5. Kits will be stored as before by 12 noon, and companies will each detail 1 man unfit for trench work as baggage guard.

6. Transport Officer will arrange limbers to take H.Q. Kits Mess Stroes and Orderly Room stores to Windy Corner.

7. Rations for 19th inst will be carried into the line and water bottles filled.

8. Stand To will be at 2.30 a.m. and 8 p.m.

                                        Capt & Adjt.
                                  19th (S(Bn The Durham L.I

Copies to
   No., 1   17th W.Yorks.
        2.   O.C. 'W' Coy.
        3.   "   'X' "
        4.   "   'Y' "
        5   "   'Z' "
        6   H.Q. No. 2 Mess.
        7.   Q.Mr and T.O.
        8.   File.

SECRET.　　　　MOVE ORDERS BY

MAJOR R.L.MASKELL TEMPY COMMANDING

19th (SERVICE) BATTALION THE DURHAM LIGHT INFANTRY.

No. 1.　　　　　20th May 1916.

1. The Battalion will be relieved in the trenches by the 17th Battn Lancashire Fusiliers on the evening of Monday, 22nd inst and will proceed to billets at FOSSE via QUEEN MARY'S Road and cross roads at N.25.a.6.5.

2. All trench stores will be handed over and receipts for same sent to Orderly Room by noon 23rd instant.

3. All movements E of the LAKE River will be by platoons at 200 yards interval and by sections S.S. of LACOUTURE.

4. One Officer per Company and 1 N.C.O per platoon of the relieving Battalion and men for patrolling will be coming into the line on 21st inst. Guides to meet these parties- 1 guide per Coy- will be at RICHEBOURG POST at 6.0P.M.

5. Relief of Lewis Guns, Signallers and Snipers will be complete by 8 a.m. on 22nd.
Guides will meet them at RICHEBOURG POST at 7 a.m. and will proceed in parties of not more than 6 at a time. Specialist Officers will detail these guides.

6. 'X' Coy 19th D.L.I. will be relieved by 'Z' Coy 17th Lanc Fus.
　'W' "　　　　-do-　　"　"　"　"　'W' "　　-do-
　'Z' "　　　　-do-　　"　"　"　"　'X' "　　-do-
　'Y' "　　　　-do-　　"　"　"　"　'Y' "　　-do-

7. Guides, under Lt C.S.Pearson for Companies in front line, and also for posts and H.Q.Coy will be at RICHEBOURG POST at 8 P.M. 22nd.

8. Order of marching out will be as follows:-
　Centre. Left. Right. Support.

9. C.Q.M.Sergeants will meet companies on arrival.

　　　　　　　　　　　　　E Cameron
　　　　　　　　　　　　　Capt & Adjt.
　　　　　　　　　　　　　19th (S) Bn the Durham Light I.

Copies to
'W' Coy.
'X' "
'Y' "
'Z' "
Lewis Gun Officer.
War Diary.
File.

19th (S) BATTALION THE DURHAM LIGHT INFANTRY.

S E C R E T.   28-5-16.   4 a.m.

1. The 106th Infantry Brigade will be prepared to relieve the 118th Infantry Brigade in the FESTUBERT Section on the shortest possible notice.

2. The 19th (S) Bn The Durham Light Infantry will relieve the 1/1st Cambridgeshire Regiment at LE TOURET (H.Q. X.16.)

3. If at night the Battalion will march as a whole "Z" Coy leading and forming an advanced guard. If by day companies will move by sections at 200 yards interval.

4. Route. La Fosse- R.22.a.8.5.- R.35.a.5.0. - LACAUTURE-
            EMPEROR'S ROAD-LE TOURET.
   Guides will meet the Battalion at X.16.d.3.9.

5. 1 N.C.O. per Company and 1 man per billet will be left behind in charge of such baggage &c., as can not be moved with the Battalion.

6. Cookers will accompany their companies.

7. On orders to move Lieut Mundy will proceed at once on bicycle and report to Brigade Major 118th Brigade. (Bde H.Q. X.28.a.3.7) and will then proceed to new billets at LE TOURET.

8. All sotred &c will be taken over and lists forwarded to the Orderly Room as soon as possible.

9. Dress. Marching Order without packs, packet haversacks, and steel helmets on back, rolled waterproof capes.

                                            Capt & Adjt.
                                    19tj (S) Bn The Durham Light Infantry

VOL 5

Army Form C. 2118

WAR DIARY
INTELLIGENCE SUMMARY

of 19th (S) Battalion
The Durham Light Infantry
for month of JUNE - 1916.

(Erase heading not required.)

Place	Date	Hour	Summary of Events and Information	Remarks and references to Appendices
LE TOURET In the Trenches	1		Battalion relieved 17th West Yorkshire Regt. in left sub-sector "Fauburt" Section in the trenches, without incident.	
"	2		Situation normal	
"	3		-do-	
"	4		-do-	
"	5			
LE TOURET.	6		Battalion relieved by 17th West Yorkshire Regt. + relief completed without incident.	
"	7		Battalion in billets	
"	8		-do-	
"	9		-do-	
"	10		-do-	
FOSSE	11		Battalion relieved in billets by 16th Notts + Derby Regt. and proceeded to billets in FOSSE.	
	12		Battalion in billets	
	13		-do-	
	14		-do-	
	15		-do-	
GONNEHEM	16		Battalion moved into "Corps reserve" to billets at GONNEHEM.	
	17		Battalion in billets	
	18		-do-	
	19		-do-	
	20		-do-	
	21		-do-	
	22		-do-	
	23		-do-	
	24		-do-	
	25		-do-	
	26		-do-	
	27		-do-	
	28		-do-	
	29		-do-	
	30		-do-	

19th (S) Bn The Durham. L.I.
War Diary.

Appendix 1
2nd June 1916
Lt C W Pollock reported for duty from 3rd Battn Durham. L.I. and was posted to 'W' Company.

Appendix 2
6th June 1916.
2 Lt W Braidford reported for duty from 3rd Battn Durham L.I. and was posted to 'Y' Company.

Appendix 3
11th June 1916.
2 Lt K Smith reported for duty from 17th Bn. Durham L.I. and was posted to 'Z' Coy.

Appendix 4
22nd June 1916.
2 Lt. G.B. Chester reported for duty from 3rd Battalion Durham L.I. and was posted to 'W' Company.
2 Lt P.V. French reported for duty from 3rd Battalion Durham L.I. and was posted to X Company.

Appendix 5
23rd June 1916.
2 Lt. L Brotherton reported for duty from 3rd Battalion Durham Light Infantry and was posted to 'W' Company.
2 Lt S. H Smith reported for duty from 16th Battalion Durham Light Infantry and was posted to 'Y' Company.
2 Lt. T H Moorwood reported for duty from 16th Battalion Durham Light Infantry and was posted to X Company.

Appendix 6
25th June 1916.
2 Lt L Millar reported for duty from 17th Battalion Durham L.I. and was posted to 'Z' Coy.

E Jameson Capt.
Adjt 19 D.L.I

106th Bde.
35th Div.

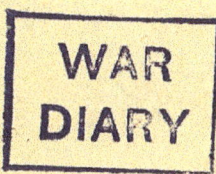

19th BATTALION

DURHAM LIGHT INFANTRY

1st to 31st JULY 1916.

Report on Operations 29/30th July with G.S. Diary

35

Army Form C. 2118

of 19th (S) Battalion The Durham L.I.
for the month of July 1916.

Vol 6

WAR DIARY
— or —
INTELLIGENCE SUMMARY
(Erase heading not required.)

Instructions regarding War Diaries and Intelligence Summaries are contained in F.S. Regs., Part II. and the Staff Manual respectively. Title Pages will be prepared in manuscript.

Place	Date 1916	Hour	Summary of Events and Information	Remarks and references to Appendices
GONNEHEM	July 1		Battn in billets	
"	" 2		Entrained at CHOCQUES about 10·30 P.M.	
"	" 3		Detrained at FREVENT about 2·30 A.M. & marched to billets at LE SOUICH	
LE SOUICH	" 4		Battn in billets	
"	" 5		Marched to Bois du WARNIMONT	
"	" 6		Arrived at – above – at 2·30 P.M.	
"	" 7		In bivouac Bois du WARNIMONT	
"	" 8		— do —	
"	" 9		— do —	
"	" 10		Marched to VARENNES via a wood due South of Bm BEAUSSART (Maps of: FRANCE – LENS – 1/– Tigers)	
"	" 11		In billets VARENNES	
"	" 12		Left for BRESLE about 6·0 P.M. & arrived 11·30 P.M.	
"	" 13		Left for Bois de TRILLES & thence in the evening to BILLON COPSE & bivouaced overnight	
"	" 14		Marched to TALUS BOISÉ & bivouaced overnight	
"	" 15		Left 4 A.M. for trenches running E & W just behind MONTAUBAN	
"	" 16		In same trenches	
"	" 17		In same trenches	
"	" 18		At 7·0 P.M. left above position to re-inforce 26th Brigade in LONGUEVAL village & DELVILLE wood. Its instructions in writing were handed to Major E.F. OSLER commanding the Battn in absence of Lt Col. STONEY who was sick and were as follows, viz:–	

WAR DIARY CONTINUED of 19th (S) Batt. The Durham L.I.
or
INTELLIGENCE SUMMARY for month of JULY - 1916
(Erase heading not required.)

Army Form C. 2118

Place	Date	Hour	Summary of Events and Information	Remarks and references to Appendices
	July	18	To 19th D.L.I. - FRANK. —	
			Sudden no 26/1559 - day of month 18/7.	
			19th D.H. will move to LONGUEVAL to reinforce	
			the remaining units of 26th/B & assist to regain over	
			old positions gradually care being taken that the flanks are well protected aaa O/c 19th D.H. will	
			Report to O/c 10th A.& S.H. aaa Touch with 18th Div. must be maintained throughout at S-18-C-5-7. aaa	
			Every effort is to be made to finally re-occupy DELVILLE wood which is to be held at all costs.	
			6-15 P.M. ROME. (signed) J.S. Brent Maj. B/M.	
	"	19	In village and wood.	
	"	20	Batt relieved by Royal Scots Fusiliers at 2-0 A.M. and returned to Camp at CAFTET WOOD	
	"	21	Working party of 300 men sent from CAFTET WOOD to work between TRONES WOOD and WATERLOT FARM.	
	"	22	In Camp at CAFTET WOOD	
	"	23	— do —	
	"	24	at 1-0 A.M. left for position N.W. of BERNAFAY WOOD S-22-d- in support of 9th Div: (Ref Trench map 1/10,000	
	"	25	Remained in same position until 6-30 P.M. evening of 26th when relieved by the 23rd Royal Fusiliers LONGUEVAL S7C.S.W.3)	
			and returned to Camp at CAFTET WOOD.	
	"	26	In camp at CAFTET WOOD and at 8-30 P.M. left for SILESIA TRENCH A. 10-C- (Ref 62. C.N.W.1)	
	"	27	Still in SILESIA TRENCH 1/10,000	
	"	28	— do —	
	"	29	— do —	

Army Form C. 2118

WAR DIARY CONTINUED of 19th (S) Battn. The Durham L.I. for July 1916.
INTELLIGENCE SUMMARY
(Erase heading not required.)

Instructions regarding War Diaries and Intelligence Summaries are contained in F. S. Regs., Part II. and the Staff Manual respectively. Title Pages will be prepared in manuscript.

Place	Date	Hour	Summary of Events and Information	Remarks and references to Appendices
	July 30	4-45 A.M.	attached to 89th Brigade and in support of to them in "general attack" on Malz Horn Farm and Guillemont.	
		7-30 P.M.	Proceeded to position S. of Trones Wood and remained there until 8-30 P.M. when ordered to return to Caftet Wood.	
	31		Left Caftet Wood at 9-0 A.M. for Sand Pit Valley.	
			Approximate casualties during above period 12 officers and 250 O.R.	

E Hanster Capt
act 19 DLI
adj

WAR DIARY

Appendix 1.
15th July 1916

2/Lt.A.S.Carroll wounded

Appendix 2.
17th July 1916

Lieut.Jas.Phillips wounded

Appendix 3.
18th July 1916

2/Lt.L.Millar killed, Capt.J.W.Waller and 2/Lt.R.Heaton wounded.

Appendix 4.
19th July 1916

2/Lt.P.V.French died of wounds, 2/Lt.W.F.Reeve, Lieut.J.Mundy, and Capt.R.C.Taylor, all wounded

Appendix 5.
22nd July 1916

Major S.Huffam from 17th.(s) Bn.West Yorkshire Regt. assumed temporary command vice Lt.Col.L.S.Stoney sick.

Appendix 7.
23rd July 1916

2/Lts.C.M.Pope and C.F.Drabble reported for duty from 16th.D.L.I. and were posted to 'Y' and 'W' Coys. respectively. Lieut. C.W.Pollock wounded.

Appendix 8.
24th July 1916

2/Lt.W.Bradford killed, 2/Lt.S.H.Smith wounded.

Appendix 8.
27th July 1916

83 other ranks arrived from Base and were taken on the strength of the Battalion.

Appendix 9.
28th July 1916

Lieut.H.C.V.Hall reported for duty from 21st.D.L.I. and was posted to W Coy.
Lieut.P.W.Day reported for duty from 21st.D.L.I. and was posted to X Coy.
2/Lt.R.A.Wilson reported for duty from 16th.D.L.I. and was posted to Z Coy.
2/Lt.R.F.Spalding reported for duty from 16th.D.L.I. and was posted to Y.Coy.
2/Lt.R.M.Middleton reported for duty from 16th.D.L.I. and was posted to H.Q.Coy.
2/Lt.J.C.Corringham reported for duty from 17th.D.L.I. and was posted to Z.Coy.

10 other ranks arrived from 15th.Notts and Derby Regt.

Capt. & Adj.
19th.D.L.I

106th Infantry Brigade.
35th Division.

1/19th BATTALION

DURHAM LIGHT INFANTRY

AUGUST 1916

35/[?]

Army Form C. 2118

Of the 19th (S) Battalion
The Durham Light Infantry
for August, 1916.

WAR DIARY
INTELLIGENCE SUMMARY
(Erase heading not required.)

Instructions regarding War Diaries and Intelligence Summaries are contained in F. S. Regs., Part II. and the Staff Manual respectively. Title Pages will be prepared in manuscript.

Place	Date	Hour	Summary of Events and Information	Remarks and references to Appendices
	Aug 1		Battn. left Sand Pit Valley for MORLANCOURT & arrived there at 8.0 P.M.	
	2		At MORLANCOURT.	
	3		" MORLANCOURT.	
	4		" at MORLANCOURT.	
	5		Marched to MÉRICOURT Station & entrained. Detrained at SALEUX and marched from there to FOURDRINOY.	Arrived 11-0 p.m.
	6		Battn. at FOURDRINOY	
	7		-- do --	
	8		-- do --	
	9		-- do --	
	10		Marched to HANGEST and entrained. Detrained MÉRICOURT. Marched to MORLANCOURT, arrived midnight.	
	11		At MORLANCOURT	
	12		-- do --	
	13		-- do --	
	14		-- do --	
	15		-- do --	
	16		-- do --	
	17		Left MORLANCOURT, marched to SAND PIT VALLEY.	
	18		At SAND PIT VALLEY	
	19		-- do --	
	20		Battn. moved to bivouacs in position S. of CAFTET WOOD.	
	21		Same position	
	22		Battn. marched to trenches on Eastern slope of MALZ HORN ridge and relieved 2nd Manchester Regt., relief being complete about midnight.	

(Continued)

Army Form C. 2118.

WAR DIARY continued of 19th (S) Battn. The Durham Lght Infantry for month of August 1916

INTELLIGENCE SUMMARY

(Erase heading not required.)

Place	Date	Hour	Summary of Events and Information	Remarks and references to Appendices
	Aug 23		Battn. in trenches. Heavy shelling by enemy causing numerous casualties	
	24		Battalion remained in trenches until the evening when relieved by 17th West Yorkshire Regt. Relief being complete about midnight	
	25		After relief in trenches battn. moved to SILESIA TRENCH arriving about 3.0 A.M.	
	26		Marched to HAPPY VALLEY	
	27		At HAPPY VALLEY	
	28		----- do -----	
	29		----- do -----	
	30		Marched to HEILLY Station & entrained. Detrained CANDAS Stn & marched to VACQUERIE and EPECAMPS	
	31		Left VACQUERIE and EPECAMPS and marched to BEAUDRICOURT to billets.	

Approximate Casualties during MALZ HORN ridge operations
Officers 3.
O.R. 110.

E Emerson Capt
adjt 19 DLI

War Diary.

Appendix 1.
5.8.16
2/Lt G M Drabble left Battalion for duty as Observer with Royal Flying Corps.

Appendix 2.
16.8.16
Draft of 24 men arrived from Base.

Appendix 3
17.8.16
2/Lt S F Bates reported for duty from 17th D.L.I and was posted to 'X' Coy.
2/Lt W E Harding reported for duty from 17th D.L.I and was posted to 'Z' Coy

Appendix 4
27.8.16
Draft of 40 men arrived from Base.

Appendix 5
31.8.16
2/Lt W H Watson reported for duty from 23rd D.L.I. and was posted to X Coy.
2/Lt E Welbourne reported for duty from 17th D.L.I and was posted to 'Z' Coy.

E Hamilton
Captain & Adjt
19th Durham L.I

Vol 8

Army Form C. 2118

WAR DIARY for September: 19th (S) Battalion
or
INTELLIGENCE SUMMARY
The Durham Light Infantry

(Erase heading not required.)

Instructions regarding War Diaries and Intelligence Summaries are contained in F. S. Regs., Part II. and the Staff Manual respectively. Title Pages will be prepared in manuscript.

Place	Date	Hour	Summary of Events and Information	Remarks and references to Appendices
	1	Sept	At BEAUDRICOURT.	
	2	"	Marched from BEAUDRICOURT to SUS ST LEGER, thence by lorries to AGNEZ.	
	3	"	Marched from AGNEZ to ARRAS. Batt. went into Brigade reserve.	
	4	"	ARRAS in billets, one company at ST NICHOLAS, one in ROCLINCOURT, one in THELUS and OBSERVATORY redoubts.	
	5	"	—do—	
	6	"	—do—	
	7	"	—do—	
	8	"	—do—	
	9	"	—do—	
	10	"	Moved into trenches in K.2 sector, relieving 18th Highland L.I. during morning, relief completed without incident.	
	11	"	—do—	
	12	"	—do—	
	13	"	—do—	
	14	"	—do—	
	15	"	—do—	
	16	"	Relieved by 18th Highland L.I. in ARRAS, leaving there same evening 8 p.m. for PUISSANS at PUISSANS in billets, Battalion being in Divisional reserve.	
	17	"	—do—	
	18	"	—do—	
	19	"	—do—	
	20	"	—do—	
	21	"	Left PUISSANS at 6-30 p.m. marched to billets in ARRAS.	
	22	"	Moved into trenches in K.2 sector, relieving 18th Highland L.I. during morning relief completed without incident.	
	23	"	—do—	
	24	"	—do—	
	25	"	—do—	
	26	"	—do—	
	27	"	—do—	
	28	"	Relieved by 18th Highland L.I. and moved into billets in ARRAS, Battalion in Brigade reserve.	
	29	"	In billets in ARRAS, one company at ST NICHOLAS, one in ROCLIN COURT, one in THELUS and OBSERVATORY redoubts.	
	30	"	—do—	

Cameron Capt
Sept 19

Army Form C. 2118

WAR DIARY for October, 1916. VO&9
or
INTELLIGENCE SUMMARY 19th (S) Batt.
(Erase heading not required.) The Durham Light Infantry

Instructions regarding War Diaries and Intelligence Summaries are contained in F. S. Regs., Part II. and the Staff Manual respectively. Title Pages will be prepared in manuscript.

Place	Date	Hour	Summary of Events and Information	Remarks and references to Appendices
	Oct 1		Battalion in Brigade Reserve, H.Q. and one Company in ARRAS, One Company at St NICHOLAS, one at ROCLINCOURT, one in PELON R3.	
	2	"	-do-	-do-
	3	"	-do-	-do-
	4	"	-do-	-do-
	5		Relieved 18th Highland L.I. in trenches in K.2. sub-sector during the afternoon. Relief completed without incident.	
	6		In trenches in K.2. sub-sector.	
	7	"	-do-	
	8	"	-do-	
	9	"	-do-	Carried out successful discharge of gas about 9.0 P.M.
	10			
	11		Battalion relieved by 18th Highland L.I. during the morning & went into Divisional Reserve in ARRAS.	
	12		In Divisional Reserve.	
	13	"	-do-	
	14	"	-do-	
	15	"	-do-	
	16	"	-do-	
	17		Relieved 18th Highland L.I. in the trenches in K.2. sub-sector during the morning. Relief completed without incident.	
	18		In trenches in K.2. sub-sector.	
	19	"	-do-	
	20	"	-do-	
	21	"	-do-	
	22	"	-do-	
	23		Battalion relieved by 18th Highland L.I. and moved into Brigade Reserve, one Company ARRAS, one St NICHOLAS, one ROCLINCOURT and one in PELON R3.	
	24		In Brigade Reserve	
	25	"	-do-	
	26	"	-do-	
	27	"	-do-	
	28	"	-do-	
	29		Battalion relieved 15th Highland L.I. in K.2. sub-sector during the morning. Relief complete without incident.	
	30		In the trenches	
	31	"	-do-	

E. Lancier Capt
Oct 19 D.L.I. 7/2

APPENDIX.

Appendix 1.   Draft of 5 men arrived from the Base.
2-10-16.

Appendix 2.   Draft of 12 men arrived from the Base.
11-10-16.

Appendix 3.   Draft of 7 men reported from the Base.
19-10-16.

Appendix 4.   Lieut J Mundy reported to the Battalion for duty
19-10-16.   and was posted to 'Z' Company.

Cameron
Captain & Adjutant.
19th (S) Bn The Durham Light Inf.

Army Form C. 2118

WAR DIARY
of 19th (S) Battalion
INTELLIGENCE SUMMARY
The Durham L.I. for
NOVEMBER 1916

Vol XI 10

(Erase heading not required.)

Instructions regarding War Diaries and Intelligence Summaries are contained in F.S. Regs., Part II. and the Staff Manual respectively. Title Pages will be prepared in manuscript.

Place	Date	Hour	Summary of Events and Information	Remarks and references to Appendices
Nov'r	1.		Battalion in the trenches in K.2. sub-sector.	
	2.		-do-	
	3.		-do-	
	4.		Battalion relieved during the morning by 18th Highland L.I. & went into Divisional reserve billets ARRAS.	
	5.		In billets	
	6.		-do-	
	7.		-do-	
	8.		-do-	
	9.		-do-	
	10.		Marched out of Divisional reserve billets & relieved the 18th Highland L.I. in the trenches in K.2. sub-sector.	
	11.		Battalion in trenches in K.2. sub-sector	
	12.		-do-	
	13.		-do-	
	14.		-do-	
	15.		-do-	
	16.		-do-	
	17.		Battalion relieved by 18th Highland L.I.; two companies going into "WORKS" line, one to BOISINCOURT and one to St NICHOLAS in Brigade reserve.	
	18.		Battalion in Brigade reserve	
	19.		-do-	
	20.		-do-	
	21.		-do-	
	22.		-do-	
	23.		Battalion relieved 18th Highland L.I. in the trenches in K.2. sub-sector, during the morning.	
	24.		Battalion in the trenches	
	25.		-do-	
	26.		At about 2.15 P.M. the enemy raided the trenches occupied by L. Coy on the right of the line in the vicinity of "KING CRATER" killing LtWM wounding Lt MUNDY and 2/Lt HARDING	

WAR DIARY

Army Form C. 2118

continued 19th (S) Battalion
The DURHAM Light Infantry
for NOVEMBER 1916

INTELLIGENCE SUMMARY

(Erase heading not required.)

Place	Date	Hour	Summary of Events and Information	Remarks and references to Appendices
Novr	26.		and 3 O.R. and taking prisoner 1 O.R. Lt MUNDY since died of wounds. The counter attack platoon under Lt HOWES moved up to drive the enemy out & found the trenches had been vacated by him. At 3.0 P.M. a raiding party of 4 officers & 58 O.R. took part in a raid on the enemy trenches at the point of entry A.29.b.9.9. Two officers 2/Lt JOHNSON and 2/Lt K SMITH and 40 O.R. getting into the enemy trenches without opposition & bombed several dug-outs. They encountered none of the enemy. Our casualties were 2/Lt G WELBOURNE and 8 O.R. wounded and 2 O.R. killed, mainly by our own bombardment.	
	27. 28.		Battalion in the trenches	
	29.		Battalion relieved by 18th Highland L.I. during the morning & moved into Divisional reserve billets in ARRAS.	
	30.		Battalion in billets	
			do	

E. Lawton Capt
Adjt 19 DLI

8½/½

APPENDIX.

Appendix 1. Major B.E.Sharp transferred to 19th.N.F.
1/11/16   Draft of 12 casuals reported from Base.

Appendix 2. Lieut.J.M.Roberts transferred to M.G.C.
8/11/16

Appendix 3. Draft of 8 casuals reported from Base.
9/11/16

Appendix 4. 2/Lt.W.E.Harding reported for duty and
17/11/16   was posted to "Z" Coy.

Appendix 5. Lieut.Jas.Mundy died of wounds.
26/11/16   2/Lt.W.E.Harding and 2/Lt.E.Welbourne
             both wounded.

Appendix 6. Lieut.J.Blenkinsop reported from 22nd.
27/11/16   D.L.I. for duty as transport officer.

Appendix 7. 2/Lt.W.G.Wiseman to hospital.
29/11/16   2/Lt.T.H.Meerweed transferred to R.F.C.

E.Jamieson Capt
Adjt 19 DLI 8/12/16

Army Form C. 2118

WAR DIARY
INTELLIGENCE SUMMARY

of 19th (S) Battalion The Durham L.I. for DECEMBER 1916

Vol XI

(Erase heading not required.)

Place	Date	Hour	Summary of Events and Information	Remarks and references to Appendices
Dec	1		Battalion in Divisional Reserve in ARRAS	
	2		" relieved by 27th Inf Bde (12th R.Scots) — Bn in billets in ARRAS for working parties	
	3		Battalion in billets in ARRAS for working parties	
	4		— do —	
	5		— do —	
	6		— do —	
	7		— do —	
	8		— do —	
	9		— do —	
	10		— do —	
	11		— do —	
	12		— do —	
	13		— do —	
	14		— do —	
	15		— do —	
	16		— do —	
	17		— do —	
	18		— do —	
	19		— do —	
	20		— do —	
	21		— do —	
	22		— do —	
	23		— do —	
	24		— do —	
	25		— do —	
	26		— do —	
	27		— do —	
	28		Battalion relieved by 18th H.L.I. in evening — Battalion in billets at MAISNIL ST POL.	
	29		— do — in billets at MAISNIL ST POL	
	30		— do —	
	31		— do —	

R.M. Middleton
2/Lt & Adjt
19th D.L.I. 27.

Army Form C. 2118

WAR DIARY
or
INTELLIGENCE SUMMARY

(Erase heading not required.)

19 D.L.I

Vol 12

Instructions regarding War Diaries and Intelligence Summaries are contained in F. S. Regs., Part II. and the Staff Manual respectively. Title Pages will be prepared in manuscript.

Place	Date 1917 Jan.	Hour	Summary of Events and Information	Remarks and references to Appendices
	1		Battalion in billets at MAISNIL S POL	
	2		do	
	3		do	
	4		do	
	5		do	
	6		do	
	7		do	
	8		do	
	9		do	
	10		do	
	11		do	
	12		do	
	13		do	
	14		do	
	15		do	
	16		do	
	17		do	
	18		do	
	19		do	
	20		do	
	21		do	
	22		do	
	23		do	
	24		do	
	25		do	
	26		do	
	27		do	
	28		do	
	29		do	
	30		do	
	31		do	

APPENDIX.

Appendix 1. Lt A.S.Carroll rejoined from England and posted to 'Z' Co.
9.1.17.   2/Lt W.McBay joined from 6th D.L.I. and posted to 'Y' Co.

Appendix 2. A Draft of 8 casuals arrived.
10.1.17.

Appendix 3. A Draft of 55 O.R. arrived.
12.1.17.

Appendix 4. A Draft of 144 O.R. arrived.
14.1.17.

Appendix 5. 2/Lt J.Robertson joined from 3rd H.L.I. and posted to 'X' Co.
15.1.17.   " W.Gray   "   "   "   "   "   "   "   " 'Y' Co.

Appendix 6. A Draft of 115 O.R. arrived.
16.1.17.

Appendix 7. 2/Lt W.G.Legat joined and posted to 'W' Co.
21.1.17.   " R.H.Wright "   "   "   " 'Z' Co.

Appendix 8. 2/Lt E.L.H.Jones joined and posted to 'X' Co.
23.1.17.

19th D.L.I.

Army Form C. 2118

WAR DIARY
or
INTELLIGENCE SUMMARY
(Erase heading not required.)

of the 19th (s) Bn. the Durham Light Infantry
(Feb 1917).

Vol 13

Place	Date	Hour	Summary of Events and Information	Remarks and references to Appendices
	Feb. 1 1917		Bn. in billets at MAISNIL ST POL.	
	2		Do.	
	3		Do.	
	4		Do.	
	5		Do.	
	6		Bn. left MAISNIL ST POL and marched to BONNIÈRES and in billets there for night	
	7		Bn. BONNIÈRES and marched to HEM and in billets there for night.	
	8		Do. HEM and marched to VIGNACOURT. Bn. in billets there.	
	9		Bn. in billets, VIGNACOURT.	
	10		Do.	
	11		Do.	
	12		Do.	
	13		Do.	
	14		Do.	
	15		Do.	
	16		Do.	
	17		Do.	
	18		Do.	
	19		Bn. entrained at VIGNACOURT, and detrained at MARCELCAVE.	
	20		Bn. in billets at MARCELCAVE.	
	21		Do.	
	22		Bn. marched to CAMP DECAUVILLE and billeted in huts there.	
	23		Bn. in huts at CAMP DECAUVILLE.	
	24		Do.	
	25		Do.	

WAR DIARY (Feb. Cont'd)
INTELLIGENCE SUMMARY

Army Form C. 2118

Place	Date 1917	Hour	Summary of Events and Information	Remarks and references to Appendices
	Feb. 26		Bn. marched into Brigade Support in LIHONS Sector via CAIX and ROSIÈRES. Orderly Room in ROSIÈRES. Relief carried out without incident.	
	27		Bn. in Brigade Support LIHONS Sector – Bn. HQ. and 1 platoon in CAROLINE TRENCH 12 platoons in 1815 TRENCH. 3 platoons in rear of IRIS TRENCH. Situation normal. Bn. supplying working parties for clearing & repairing trenches.	
	28		Bn. in support. Situation normal. Work carried on as above.	

R.N. Middleton
Lieut & Adjt.
19th Bn.

3/3/17

WAR DIARY – FEBRUARY, 1917.

APPENDIX.

Appendix 1.
5. 2. 17.   Draft of 120 O.R. (Units) proceeded to BOULOGNE.
              Draft of 8 O.R. (Units) proceeded to join 26th Bn.
                 Royal Fusiliers.

Appendix 2.
7. 2. 17.   2/Lt. W.F.Reeve re-joined from England, and was posted
                 to "W" Co.

Appendix 3.
9. 2. 17.   Draft of 7 Signallers arrived from the Base.

Appendix 4.
13. 2. 17.   Draft of 2 N.C.O's arrived from the Base.

Appendix 5.
14. 2. 17.   2/Lt. M.H.McBain and 2/Lt. A.C.Paterson reported for
                 duty from 3rd D.L.I., and were posted to "Z" and
                 "X" Co.s respectively.

Appendix 6.
21. 2. 17.   2/Lt. D.C.Maclachlan was transferred to the M.G.C.
                 (Heavy Branch).

Appendix 7.
23. 2. 17.   Draft of 4 Casuals arrived from the Base.

Army Form C. 2118

WAR DIARY of the 19th (S.) Bn. The Durham Light Infantry (March 1917).

INTELLIGENCE SUMMARY

(Erase heading not required.)

Instructions regarding War Diaries and Intelligence Summaries are contained in F.S. Regs., Part II. and the Staff Manual respectively. Title Pages will be prepared in manuscript.

Vol II

Place	Date 1917	Hour	Summary of Events and Information	Remarks and references to Appendices
	Mch. 1		Bn. in Brigade Support in LIHONS SECTOR.	
	" 2		" moved up to front line of left sub-sector of LIHONS SECTOR in the evening and relieved 17th West Yorks. Relief interrupted owing to enemy shells. Raids on front line trenches by enemy in the second half in the morning of the 3rd, but captured a German prisoner who was wounded and afterwards died. The enemy captured a Machine Gun.	
	" 3		Bn. in front line of left sub-sector of LIHONS SECTOR, situation normal.	
	" 4		Do. Do.	
	" 5		Do. Do.	
	" 6		Bn. moved to Brigade Reserve ROSIÈRES, being relieved by 17th W. Yorks in the evening. We relieved 18th H.L.I. in Bde. Reserve. Relief completed without incident.	
	" 7		Bn. in Brigade Reserve ROSIÈRES. Part of Bn. working parties.	
	" 8		Do. Do.	
	" 9		Do. Do.	
	" 10		Bn. moved to front line of left sub-sector of LIHONS SECTOR in the evening and relieved 17th West Yorks. A.T.A.L.? Relief completed without incident.	
	" 11		Bn. in front line of left sub-sector of LIHONS SECTOR, situation normal.	
	" 12		Do. Do.	
	" 13		Do. Do.	
	" 14		Bn. moved into billets in ROSIÈRES for one night on Brigade being relieved by 105th Inf. Bde. Bn. relieved by 1st Gloucesters in evening. Relief completed without incident.	
	" 15		marched to CAMP DES BALLONS, near CAIX in afternoon. Bn. accommodated in huts.	
	" 16		Bn. in huts at CAMP DES BALLONS, near CAIX.	
	" 17		Bn. moved to ROSIÈRES at night, and billeted there for the night.	

WAR DIARY (contd)

Army Form C. 2118

(Erase heading not required.)

Place	Date 1917	Hour	Summary of Events and Information	Remarks and references to Appendices
	Mch. 18		Bn. moved in morning to old British front line N.E. of CHILLY, and took up position from Bois de (inclusive) to the CHILLY - MEHARICOURT Rd. inclusive, until next morning.	
	19		Bn. moved forward at 6 A.M. and occupied trenches, dug-outs and cellars at HALLU.	
	20		Bn. at HALLU and engaged in working parties, repairing roads to.	
	21		Do	
	22		Do	
	23		Do	
	24		Do	
	25		Do	
	26		Do	
	27		Do	
	28		Do	
	29		Bn. moved forward to billets, MORCHAIN.	
	30		Bn. in billets at MORCHAIN and engaged on working parties, repairing road to.	
	31		Do	

R.M. Middleton
Lieut. & Adjt.
19th Dl.

1/4/17.

APPENDIX.

Appendix 1.
1.3.17
Capt J.W. Waller rejoined from England & took over command of 'W' Co.
2/Lt. C.M. Pape transferred to 42nd P.O.W. Co.

Appendix 2
2.3.17
2/Lt. M.H. McBain reposted to 2nd D.L.I.

Appendix 3
5.3.17
Draft of 12 Casuals reposted from Base.

Appendix 4
7.3.17
Draft of 42 O.R. arrived from Base.

Appendix 5
10.3.17
Lt Col. B.C. Dent transferred to 16th Cheshires.
Major W.B. Greenwell takes over command of Bn.
2/Lt J. Blenkinsop joined from 3rd D.L.I. and posted to Z Co.

Appendix 6
11.3.17
Lieut Jas. Phillips joined from 3rd D.L.I.

Appendix 7
16.3.17
Capt. A.F. Davey posted to Establishment 3rd Army Inf. School (Authy) B/4444 of 19.10.16

Appendix 8
21.3.17
2/Lt G.F. Golightly & H. Wharton joined from 3rd D.L.I. and are posted to 'Z' Co.

Appendix 9
30.3.17
2/Lt J.R. Ozzard joined from 3rd D.L.I & is posted to Z Co.
Draft of 50 O.R. arrived from Base.

R.M. Middleton Lieut & Adjt
19 D.L.I

WAR DIARY of the 19th (S) Bn. The Durham Light Infantry.
INTELLIGENCE SUMMARY (April, 1917).

Army Form C. 2118

Vol 5

Place	Date 1917	Hour	Summary of Events and Information	Remarks and references to Appendices
	Apl 1		Bn. in billets at MORCHAIN and engaged in working parties on roads & craters in immediate vicinity.	
	2		Do.	
	3		Bn. moved forward. HQ. and 2 Co. in billet at QUIVIÈRES and 3 Co. & transport in DOUVIEUX. Bn. engaged in working parties repairing roads & in district. Specialist & infy. training.	
	4		Do.	
	5		Do.	
	6		Do.	
	7		HQ. and 2 Co. moved from QUIVIÈRES to FLEZ & are billeted there.	
	8		Bn. at FLEZ. A practice attack was made on UGNY WOOD and UGNY VILLAGE.	
	9		Bn. moved forward to TREFCON and relieved 2/6th Gloucesters 61st Div. in billets there.	
	10		Bn. moved forward and relieved 2/4th R.Berks in night Bn. 'A' Det. relieved left Bn. NW of ST QUENTIN and east of TUMULUS. Bn. HQ. at BIHÉCOURT. Co. in Bn. Reserve at VADENCOURT CHATEAU. C. in outposts just east of VADENCOURT and 2 Co. in front line on MAREVAL COPSE (old German line). Situation quiet.	
	11		Do.	
	12		Left Bn. (18th H.L.I.) withdrawn. 19th DLI becoming left Bn. and carrying up with 5 [?] Bn. on left flanks. 17th R.Scots moved into line. Our right flank linking up at the boundary line on IRON RIVER. Left front line Co. pushed out outposts. NW of TUMULUS and night Co. occupied line between PONTRU and TUMULUS supports in front C. in Bn. Reserve moved into roads between outposts just E. of VADENCOURT Co. in Bn. Reserve moved to dig in from the TUMULUS to a point NW of TUMULUS on road at about R6 d.9.9. Situation quiet.	
	13		1 Co. W Yorks relieved Co. in Bn. Reserve in road E. of VADENCOURT	

1875 Wt. W.593/826 1,000,000 4/15 J.B.C. & A. A.D.S.S./Forms/C. 2118.

Army Form C. 2118

WAR DIARY (cont.)
INTELLIGENCE SUMMARY

(Erase heading not required.)

Instructions regarding War Diaries and Intelligence Summaries are contained in F.S. Regs., Part II. and the Staff Manual respectively. Title Pages will be prepared in manuscript.

Place	Date 1917	Hour	Summary of Events and Information	Remarks and references to Appendices
	Apl. 14		Night of 14/15 Bn. relieved the 17th W. Yorks Regt except 1 C. which was left in Bde. Reserve to W. Yorks in trench just E. of VADENCOURT. Bn. moved to billets in Reserve to left Bn. in and around SOYECOURT. Relief carried out without incident.	
	15		Bn. in billets at SOYECOURT and engaged in working parties repairing roads, craters and bridges in neighbourhood.	
	16		do	
	17		do	
	18		Bn. relieved 17th W. Yorks Regt in same sector as before to occupy on the 1st of next 1 C. of W. Yorks remained in Bn. Reserve in road just E. of VADENCOURT. Relief carried out without incident.	
	19		Bn. in the line in left sub-sector of left Bde front in a line running PONTRU, TUMULUS, R6a 9.9. Situation quiet. Less shelling than previous two twenty	
	20		do do do do few casualties	
	21		do	
	22			
	23		Bn. relieved by 23rd Manchesters and moved into billets at TREFCON into Bn Reserve at TREFCON. Relief completed without incident.	
	24		Bn. engaged in working parties. Cleaning up training in attack formations.	
	25		Bn. at TREFCON. Training attack formations.	
	26		do Bn. engaged in working parties repairing roads to in neighbourhood	
	27		do Attack scheme practised. An group between TERTRY and BEAUVOIS. Attempt to clear enemy out of BEAUVOIS	
	28		do Bn. engaged in working parties repairing roads to in neighbourhood	

Army Form C. 2118

WAR DIARY (cont.)
INTELLIGENCE SUMMARY

(Erase heading not required.)

Place	Date 1917	Hour	Summary of Events and Information	Remarks and references to Appendices
	Apl.	29	Bn. at TREFCON. B. training and bathing. Attack formation practiced	
	"	30	do. Specialists under training. Tank Bn. engaged in working parties in morning referring roads to Bn. moved forward at night and relieved the 15th Sherwoods in Bde. Reserve to Right Bn. in Right Bde. Sector, 3 Co. in sunken road SW of FRESNOY-LE-PETIT and HQ. and Co. in Bn. Reserve at MAISON DU GARDE, BOIS D'HOLNON.	

R.R. Middleton
Lieut. + adjt.
19th D.L.I.

Appendix to War Diary

Appendix 1 — Draft of 1 casual arrived from Base
2.4.17 — Lt J Phillips transferred to 2/5th Gloucester Regt as Transport Officer

Appendix 2 — 2/Lt T E Haddon reported on 1st appointment
3.4.17 — & posted to W Co

Appendix 3 — 2/Lt Day wounded
13.4.17 — 2/Lt G B Chester

Appendix 4 — 2/Lts J Gardner & W Iley reported from
15.4.17 — Base & posted to W & X Cos respectively

Appendix 5 — Major D Huffam took over temporary
16.4.17 — command of 17th R. Scots

Appendix 6 — Draft of 8 men arrived from Base.
18.4.17

Appendix 7 — Capt C E S Gates cross-posted from
21.2.17 — 16th Ches R

Appendix 8 — Lt J Rozzard wounded
22.4.17

Appendix 9 — Draft of 6 arrived from the
24.4.17 — Base.

Appendix 10. 2/Lts B A Taylor & C Pugh rejoined
29/4/7   from Base & are posted to X
          & Y Coy respectively.

                                    Lieut & Adjt
                                    19th O N I

30/4/17

Army Form C. 2118

Instructions regarding War Diaries and Intelligence Summaries are contained in F. S. Regs., Part II. and the Staff Manual respectively. Title Pages will be prepared in manuscript.

WAR DIARY
or
INTELLIGENCE SUMMARY

of the 19th (S) Bn. The Durham Light Infantry. (May 1917)

(Erase heading not required.)

Place	Date	Hour	Summary of Events and Information	Remarks and references to Appendices
FRESNOY SECTOR	May	1	Bn. in support to right Bn. (19th W. Yorks.) of right Brigade (146th) front in Bois D'MOIRON. 3 Cos. in sunken road SW of FRESNOY LE PETIT. B. HQ and a Co. in reserve in "Brown's Line" of resistance. near MAISON DE GARDE. Bn. engaged at night working on "Brown's Line" of resistance.	
		2	do.	
		3	do.	
		4	Bn. relieved 17th West Yorks. at night. 2 Co. in front line & posts, one in "Brown's Line" and one in sunken road SW of FRESNOY LE PETIT. Bn. HQ. in Quarry off road about M.27.a.o.5. (62 S SW.) Relief completed without incident.	
		5	Raid on LES TROIS SAUVAGES M.23.b. and an enemy trench near by 2 Co. (Y and Z). Zero was at 12.30 am and the Co. had artillery support but unsuccessful owing to large enemy occupation. Our casualties were approximately 3 officers & 58 OR. The left front line Co. (W) in conjunction with raiding party was successful in establishing useful advanced posts N.W of LES TROIS SAUVAGES in M.23.a.	
		6	Bn. in the line. Situation normal.	
		7	do.	
		8	Bn. was relieved at night by 15th Sherwood Foresters, 105th Bde. Just prior to relief posts established on night 7/8th were driven in by the enemy. Relief completed without incident. Bn. moved into Divisional Reserve in tents at TREFCON.	
		9	Bn. in camp at TREFCON. Cleaning up & checking kit &c during day.	
		10	do. Past Bn. repairing roads in the district remainder training mostly formation, specialist training, musketry, range practice & route marches.	
		11	do.	
		12	do.	
		13	do.	

WAR DIARY (contd.)
INTELLIGENCE SUMMARY

Army Form C. 2118

(Erase heading not required.)

Place	Date 1917	Hour	Summary of Events and Information	Remarks and references to Appendices
	May	14	Bn. in Camp at TREFCON. Part Bn. repairing roads in the district, remainder training in attack formations, specialist training, musketry, range practice & bomb throwing.	See Hours Show
		15	do.	
		16	do.	See Hours Show
		17	do.	
		18	do.	
		19	Bn. marched with Brigade to PERONNE. Bn. in billets at PERONNE.	
		20	Bn. in billets at PERONNE. "W" Co. proceeded to TEMPLEUX LA FOSSE to erect huts for Bn.	
		21	Bn. marched with Brigade to TEMPLEUX LA FOSSE. Bn. in camp there.	
		22	Bn. in camp at TEMPLEUX LA FOSSE.	
		23	Bn. marched by road in evening and relieved the 11th Yorks Regt (40th Div) in Brigade support in billets at VILLERS GUISLAIN. Relief completed without incident.	
		24	Bn. in support at VILLERS GUISLAIN. At night engaged in working parties with 178th Tunnelling Co. and 205th Co. R.E's.	
		25	do.	
		26	do.	
		27	do.	
		28	Bn. relieved 17th W. Yorks (Left front line Bn.) right Bde Sector E. of VILLERS GUISLAIN. Relief Completed without incident.	
		29	Bn. in front line. situation normal.	
		30	do.	
		31	do. Brigade boundary altered on the left flank as follows:- New X5.a central along road X3.c.60.15 - X8.d.8.9 along track to CHAPEL CROSSING, VILLERS GUISLAIN. New latked on Bn. frontage and our left front support Co. were relieved by 2 Co. of the 18th Lanc Fusiliers. Relief completed without incident.	

R.M. Middleton
Lieut & Adjt
19th D.L.I.

Appendix to War Diary.

Appendix 1
1-5-17.
2/Lt G.W. Berry reported for duty from Base & is posted to "X" Coy.
Draft of 8 casuals from Base

Appendix 2
3rd May
2/Lt T. Blenkinsop reported missing, believed killed.
2/Lt G.J. Golightly wounded & died of wounds on the 7th May
2/Lt W. Gray wounded

Appendix 3
12th May.
Draft of 1 casuals from Base

Appendix 4
25th May
Draft of 11 Casuals from Base

19TH (S) BATTALION, DURHAM LIGHT INFANTRY.

WAR DIARY

INTELLIGENCE/SUMMARY

of the 19th (S) Bn. The Durham Light Infantry.
(June 1917)

Army Form C. 2118

Place	Date June	Hour	Summary of Events and Information	Remarks and references to Appendices
		1	Bn. in front line left Bn. front, right Bn. sub sector VILLERS GUISLAIN, situation normal	
		2	Bn. relieved by 14th Gloucesters in evening. Bn. moved into our Reserve Camp in D 18 c near AIZECOURT LE BAS. Relief completed without incident.	
		3	Bn. at rest.	
		4	Bn. cleaning up and re equipping.	
		5	Bn. in training, sports in the evening	
		6	Do.	
		7	Do.	
		8	Do.	
		9	Do.	
		10	Bn. moved in Brigade Reserve at W16a in GAUCHE Sector relieving 17th Lanc. Fus. Relief completed without incident	
		11	Bn. in Brigade Reserve, Working parties digging tr. in "Brien" line each night	
		12	Do.	
		13	Do.	
		14	Bn. moved to front line, right Bn. front, left Bn. sub. sector GAUCHE sector + relieved 17th W. Yorks. Bn. HQ. in sunken road near Cemetery in W.3. Relief completed without incident.	
		15	Bn. in front line Situation quiet	
		16	Do.	
		17	Do.	
		18	Do.	
		19	Do.	
		20	Do.	
		21	Bn. relieved by 17th W. Yorks + moved into camp in Brigade Reserve at W16a Relief completed without incident.	
		22		

Army Form C. 2118

WAR DIARY
or
INTELLIGENCE SUMMARY (cont'd) June 1917
(Erase heading not required.)

Place	Date	Hour	Summary of Events and Information	Remarks and references to Appendices
	June	23	Bn. in Brigade Reserve at W.16.a. 250 men engaged at night in digging a French in front of our front line in R.35.b.	
		24	Bn. in Brigade Reserve. Engaged at night in digging to in "Green" line.	
		25	Do. Engaged in completing a for as possible work commenced on 23rd.	
		26	Bn. relieved by 15th Sherwoods and moved to Bde Reserve in Camp W.15.a. Relief completed /without incident/	
		27	Bn. in Bde Reserve. Working parties during day.	
		28	Do.	
		29	Do.	
		30	Do.	

R.N. Middleton
Lieut & adjt
19th D.L.I.

Appendix to
War Diary.

Appendix 1
3.6.17 — Draft of 64 OR arrived from Base.

Appendix 2
6.6.17 — Capt C.E.S Noakes and 2/Lt J Robertson accidently wounded premature bomb.

Appendix 3
12.6.17 — Draft of 3 casuals arrived from the Base.

Appendix 4
22.6.17 — Draft of 12 casuals arrived from the Base.

R.B. Middleton
Lieut & Adjt
49 D L I

Officer Commanding,

    17th R. Scots.
    17th N.York. R.
    19th Durh. L. I.
    19th High. L. I.
    106th M. G. Co.
    106th T.M. Batt.
    204th F. Co. R.E.

    Reference to Administrative Order issued yesterday the advanced R.E. Dump at A.3.a.1.8. will be used as an emergency dump only, that is when extra work requires to be done on short notice and there is not time to send up material from Ros Dump.

    The 204th F. Co. R.E. will take over this dump and supply personnel required.

    Battalions will continue to send in daily to Brigade Headquarters by 9 a.m. indents of material required . This material will accompany transport with rations same night. If all material indented for is not avialable Battalions will be notified by Brigade.

    In order to prevent work being stopped by material indented for not being available for delivery same night, it is suggested that Battalions should have sufficient material forward to carry on the work irrespective of material demanded.

                                    L.H. Ross, Captain,
                                         Staff Captain,
                                      106th Infantry Brigade.

11.6.17.

Army Form C. 2118

WAR DIARY of the 19th (S) Bn. The Durham Light Infantry

INTELLIGENCE SUMMARY (July 1917)

(Erase heading not required.)

Instructions regarding War Diaries and Intelligence Summaries are contained in F.S. Regs., Part II. and the Staff Manual respectively. Title Pages will be prepared in manuscript.

WO 1A

Place	Date	Hour	Summary of Events and Information	Remarks and references to Appendices
	July			
	1		Bn. in Divisional Reserve. Moved from camp near HEUDICOURT to camp near AIZECOURT-LE-BAS about D.17.d.9.8.	
	2		Bn. in Divisional Reserve. Moved from camp mentioned above to camp near LONGAVESNES. 18th Lancashire Fusiliers moved into camp vacated.	
	3		Bn. training in vicinity of camp	
	4		Bn. in Camp. Brigade Tactical scheme held between TEMPLEUX LA FOSSE and LONGAVESNES	
	5		Bn. training, bathing and firing on range.	
	6		Bn. moved into Right Bn. Support in C1 Sub-Sector of Line NE of HARGICOURT and relieved the 12th Lancers and Oxford Hussars. Bn. H.Q. & 2 Cos in Quarry at F.27.c.7.d and 2 Cos in HARDY BANK. Relief completed without incident	
	7		Bn. in support. Digging & wiring in front line at night	
	8		Do	
	9		Do	
	10		Do	
	11		Do	
	12		Do	
	13		Do	
	14		Do	
	15		Bn. relieved the 17th Worcs in right Bn. front line C. out sector NE of HARGICOURT & occupied A, B + C Coys. One Co in Reserve in ORCHARD and TOINE Pal. Bn HQ in sunken road about F.22.b.3.3. Relief completed without incident.	
	16		Bn. in front line, situation normal	
	17		Do	
	18		Do	
	19		Do. During the night 19/20 after heavy T.M. & artillery bombardment of RIFLEMAN Post F.29.b.7.4 about 1500 yds NE of HARGICOURT, the enemy attempted a raid on the post in which he was unsuccessful. We fired the S.O.S. signal twice. Our casualties 26 Enemy left 2 dead near the Post and retired rifles, bayonets, bangalore torpedo &c.	

1875 [Wt. W.593/826 1,000,000 4/15 J.B.C. & A. A.D.S.S./Forms/C. 2118.

Army Form C. 2118

WAR DIARY (cont'd)

INTELLIGENCE SUMMARY

(Erase heading not required.)

Place	Date	Hour	Summary of Events and Information	Remarks and references to Appendices
	July	20	Bn. in front line, situation normal.	
		21	do	
		22	do	
		23	Bn. relieved by 14th Gloucesters and moved into Divisional Reserve occupying camp near AIZECOURT LE BAS D17 d 9.8. Relief completed without incident.	
		24	Bn. in camp. No training.	
		25	Cleaning up & re-fitting	
		26	Bn. training, range, bathing, bayonet fighting + physical training to.	
		27	do do	
		28	do do	
		29	Church parade.	
		30	Bn. training.	
		31	Cleaning up & preparing to move.	

3/8/17.

R.B. Riddell
Lieut + Adjt
19th Bn.

Appendix to War Diary

Appendix 1
1.7.17
2/Lts G.K.Prior & F.Smallman reported from Base for duty & posted to X & Z Cos respectively.

Appendix 2
5.7.17
2/Lt H. Heaton rejoined from England for duty & posted to W Co.

Appendix 3
10.7.17
Capt A.J.Davey rejoined from 3rd Army School.

Appendix 4
12.7.17
2/Lt W.S.Cauvin transferred to "Z" 35th T.M Batt.

Appendix 5
13.7.17
2/Lt J.Gardner transferred to R.F.C. on probation.

Appendix 6
14.7.17
Lt L.Brotherton wounded.

Appendix 7
23.7.17
Draft of 5. O.R. arrived from Base.

Appendix 8
27.7.17
26710 Pte G.B.Bell granted M.M. for good work 19/20th Inst.

Appendix 9
31.7.17
2/Lt C.H. Fox reported from Base and posted to W. Co.

R.M. Middleton
Lt & Adjt
19 DLI

WAR DIARY

19th (S.) Bn. The Durham Light Infantry

INTELLIGENCE SUMMARY

Army Form C. 2118

Place	Date	Hour	Summary of Events and Information	Remarks and references to Appendices
	Aug 1		Bn. moved from AIZECOURT LE BAS to the BIRDCAGE SECTOR, S.E. of EPEHY into Brigade Reserve occupying cellars and tents in LEMPIRE and RONSSOY. They relieved parts of the 15th Cheshires and 19th N.F.s without incident.	
	2		Bn. in Brigade Reserve in LEMPIRE and RONSSOY. Working parties at night.	
	3		Do. Do.	
	4		Do. Do.	
	5		Bn. relieved 17th KOYLIs in BIRDCAGE SECTOR (Brigade left sub-sector). Relief complete without incident.	
	6		Bn. in BIRDCAGE SECTOR front line. Situation normal.	
	7		Do. Do.	
	8		Do. Do.	
	9		Do. Do.	
	10		Bn. relieved by the III Corps Cyclist Bn. "W" Co. remaining in reserve to the latter. Relief completed without incident. Bn. moved into camp at VILLERS FAUCON on relief.	
	11		Bn. in camp at VILLERS FAUCON. Rest and cleaning up.	
	12		Do. Inspections.	
	13		Do. Working & carrying parties at night.	
	14		Do. Do.	
	15		Do. Do.	
	16		Do. Carrying parties at night.	
	17		Do. Do.	
	18		Do. Do.	

WAR DIARY (cont'd)
INTELLIGENCE SUMMARY

Army Form C. 2118

Place	Date	Hour	Summary of Events and Information	Remarks and references to Appendices
	Aug 19		Bn. moved to front line and relieved 18th Hr.L.I. in GILLEMONT FARM SE of EPEHY. Relief carried out without incident.	
	20		Bn. in front line. Except for a quiet although retaliation fire called for.	
	21		Do	
	22		Do	
	23		Do	
	24		The Bn. was relieved by the 18th Hr.L.I. and on relief moved into cellars in LEMPIRE, "C" remaining in CAT POST. Relief carried out without incident, so far as this Bn. was concerned. Hr.L.I. suffered casualties.	
	25		Bn. in cellars at LEMPIRE. In the early morning the enemy counter-attacked GILLEMONT FARM and re-took the ground lost by them in the 18th and also our front line trenches. Bn. was moved up to the farm and ordered to counter-attack at 7.30 p.m. to re-establish ourselves in our old front line. The objective was gained and we captured 1 heavy enemy M.G. & 2 Lewis guns & 3 Stokes guns and ammt. which the enemy captured from the Hr.L.I and T.M.B. respectively and remained in the line and took over from the Hr.L.I.	
	26		The Bn. was relieved by the 17th Royal Scots and proceeded to LEMPIRE in Brigade Reserve on relief. Relief completed without incident.	
	27		Bn. in Brigade Reserve working and wiring parties at night	
	28		Do	
	29		Do	

Army Form C. 2118

WAR DIARY
or
INTELLIGENCE SUMMARY
(Erase heading not required.)

Place	Date	Hour	Summary of Events and Information	Remarks and references to Appendices
	Aug	30	Bn. moves into GUILLEMONT FARM and relieves 17th Royal Scots. Situation quiet and relief completed without incident.	
		31	Bn. in front line, situation normal.	

R.M. Middleton
Lieut & Adjt
19th Bn.

19 Bn Durham L.I.

Appendix to War Diary

3/8/17	2/Lt R.D. Edgar joined Bn from Base
4/8/17	Draft of 4 Casuals	Ditto
11/8/17	2/Lt. R.W. Wright	Ditto
17/8/17	2/Lts Y.H. Waugh & G.E. Brown	Ditto
23/8/17	Draft of 5 Casuals	Ditto
25/8/17	Capt. G.R. Forster & 2/Lt. G.W. Berry. Killed in action.
26/8/17	Draft 140 ORs joined from Base.
27/8/17	2/Lt. G.E. Brown, Wounded.
30/8/17	Draft of 80 ORs arrived from Base

Estimated casualties for Aug — 100

R.S. Middleton
Lieut & Adjt.

3/9/17   19 Bn Durham Light Inf.

Copy No. 22

OPERATION ORDER No 96

1. ~~REF~~ "A" Coy Co. 16 M.G. Bn, 1 Sub-Section of 241 M.G.C. will co-operate in an attack on Gillemont Farm by the 16th H.L.I. on the morning of 19th August 1917.

2. **Co-operation of Force.** "D" Group "B" Section 241 Sub-Section of "D" 166th M.G.C.
    "F" — 12th M.G. Bn.
    "G" — A Sect; 273rd; 1 Sub-Section of "D" 166th M.G.C.
    and 1 Sub-Section 241 M.G.C.

3. **Barrage & Targets.** Barrage & Targets will be as laid down in Appendix "A"

4. **Schedule of Fire.** Fire will be carried out as in Appendix "B"

5. **Barometer & Thermometer, Winds.** These will be notified later by Appendix "C"

6. **Zero Hour** will be notified later.

7. **Hour of Readiness.** Guns will be laid by 8 P.M. 18/8/17. Hour of Readiness, Zero — 2 hrs.

8. **Rate of Fire.** Creeping Barrages — Intense. Standing Barrages — 1 belt per gun per 5 mins.

9. **Duration of Fire.** Zero to Zero + 90 mins

10. **Ammunition** 6,000 rounds per gun.
    Reserve to the belts 6,000 per gun
    " at Position in S.A.A. Boxes — 5,000 per gun.
    " at St. Emilie 5,000 per gun.

11. **Parade.** Units will parade at 4.15 P.M. and will move off by gun teams ½ mile intervals

12. **Route.** Route to positions is left to the discretion of Group Commanders

13. **Watches, Synchronization of.** Representative an officer will report Bde HQ at 5.15 P.M. on the 18th. One officer from HQ of D, E & F Groups will report at Batt HQ Ken Lane at 10.00 P.M. to synchronize. Further synchronization will take place at M.G. HQ F.16 c 4.8 at Zero — 2½ hours.

14. **Working Party.** The following working parties will be met at Batt HQ at F.15 d 65.75. At 9 P.M. on the 18th 1 N.C.O & 12 men for "G" group, 4 N.C.Os and 16 men for "F" Section. These will be returned on the night of 19th.

15. **Mobile Guns.** "C" Section under Lt S.W. Kinney on completion of barrage & at an hour to be notified later will advance to forward positions as under.
    1 Gun, Blunt Nose, 1 Gun Dog Trench
    1 " Duncan Post, 1 " Joyful Post.
    Ammunition & Water as previously arranged.
    Starting Party for Belt Boxes as in Para 12.
    For roles & schedule vide Appendix "D"

16. **Aircraft.** The following guns will be mounted for A.A. work at Zero + 2 hours: —
    1 Gun Basse Boulogne South, 1 Gun Lempire Central
    "D" group at F.16 c 2.0. F group at F.16 c 85.05
    G " F.22 c 45.25
    2 days Rations will be issued to "C" Section.

17. **Repulsion of Counter-attack.** Barrages for repulsion of Counter-attack will be laid down as in Appendix "H"

18. **Dispositions of 241 M.G.C.** Gun in E Post under Lt Boyle will move from the centre of the post to emplacement south end of sap F.22 c 05.40 so that it can command the valley towards the knoll. S.O.S. line M.B. 112° range 950x. Move to be completed by 8 P.M. 18th inst. Gun at "C" Post under Lt Bowie will have an S.O.S. line 66 mag. range 700x.

19. **Signals.** The following signal ground bursting will be used. S.O.S. lights. Lempire range 150 2 red & 2 white. This signal refers to Defensive fire only.

Army Form C. 2118

WAR DIARY of the 19th (S) Bn. The Durham Light Infantry.

INTELLIGENCE SUMMARY

Vol 20

(Erase heading not required.)

Instructions regarding War Diaries and Intelligence Summaries are contained in F.S. Regs., Part II. and the Staff Manual respectively. Title Pages will be prepared in manuscript.

Place	Date	Hour	Summary of Events and Information	Remarks and references to Appendices
	Sep 1917	1	Bn in front line at GILLEMONT FARM, S.E. of EPÉHY. Situation normal. Relieved by 14th Gloucesters and moved into camp at VILLERS FAUCON. Relief completed without incident.	
		2, 3, 4, 5	Bn in camp at VILLERS FAUCON resting and indulging in recreational exercise. Bathing on 3rd.	
		6	Bn moved forward in the evening and relieved the 18th L.F. in the BIRDCAGE SECTOR S.E. of EPÉHY. Relief completed without incident.	
		7, 8, 9, 10, 11	Bn in front line. Situation remarkably quiet. Eastern end of BIRDCAGE evacuated on night of 9th inst. and a new front line established.	
		12	Bn relieved by 17th W. Yorks and moved into Bde Reserve occupying PRIEL CUTTING, KILDARE, LIMERICK and MEATH POSTS, and VAUGHAN'S BANK. Relief completed without incident.	
		13, 14, 15, 16, 17	Bn in Bde Reserve, and engaged in working parties, part by day and part by night.	
		18	Bn relieved by 15th Cheshires and moved into camp at TEMPLEUX LA FOSSÉ. Relief completed without incident. The Bn. has no casualties from the 6th - 18th incl.	
		19, 20, 21, 22, 23, 24, 25	Bn in camp at TEMPLEUX LA FOSSÉ (Div Reserve). Daily training carried on including B.F. & P.T. Musketry, Bombing (live practice & dummy throwing) Lewis and specialist training. Bathing on 21st inst. The Corps Commander presented ribbons to Heroes & O.R. 2 Bde on the 22nd inst.	

1875 Wt. W593/826 1,000,000 4/15 J.B.C. & A. A.D.S.S./Forms/C. 2118.

WAR DIARY or INTELLIGENCE SUMMARY

of the 19th (S) Bn. the Durham Light Infantry.

Army Form C. 2118

(Erase heading not required.)

Place	Date 1917	Hour	Summary of Events and Information	Remarks and references to Appendices
	Sept.	26	The Battalion relieved 2nd Lancashire Fusiliers. Relief completed without incident.	
		27 / 28	Battalion in front-line at FLEECALL and GRAFTON POSTS S.E. of EPEHY. Situation very quiet.	
		29	Battalion relieved by 7th West Yorkshire Regt. & moved into Battalion support in LEMPIRE. Relief completed without incident.	
		30	Battalion in Battalion support — Working Parties engaged in improving FLEECALL & GRAFTON POSTS.	

N.V. Gorton
Lieut & A/Adjt.
19th (S) Bn. The Durham L.I.

APPENDIX TO WAR DIARY

Appendix 1   Draft of 14 casuals arrived from
6-9-17   Base.

Appendix 2   2/Lt R Smith arrived from Base &
10.9.17   posted to X Co.

Appendix 3   2/Lts J.J. Carney & C Milner arrived
11.9.17   from Base & posted to Z & Y Cos
             respectively.

Appendix 4   2/Lt R.S. Bootflower arrived from Base
14.9.17   & posted to Z Co.

Appendix 5   Draft of 8 casuals arrived from
24.9.17   Base.

Appendix 6   Draft of 120 arrived from
29.9.17   22nd Durham L.I.

Appendix 7   Draft of 2 casuals arrived
29.9.17   from Base.

                         H.A. Burton
                         Lieut & A/Adjt
                         10th D.L.I.

3. 10. 17

WAR DIARY or INTELLIGENCE SUMMARY

Army Form C. 2118.

October 1917 Vol 2

of the 19th (S) Bn.
(The Durham Light Infantry)

Place	Date 1917	Hour	Summary of Events and Information	Remarks and references to Appendices
	Oct. 1		Bn in support at LEMPIRE east of PERONNE. Bn engaged improving FLEECALL POST near the village	
	2		do do	
	3		At night Bn relieved by 7th King's Liverpool Regt and proceeded to camp at AIZECOURT-LE-BAS. Relief completed without incident.	
	4		Moved to PERONNE by motor lorry. Bn in billets at PERONNE.	
	5		Bn entrained at PERONNE and detrained at ARRAS, camp on morning of 6th.	
	6		Bn marched to MONTENESCOURT near ARRAS and billeted there.	
	7			
	8			
	9		Bn in billets at MONTENESCOURT. Intensive training carried on daily.	
	10			
	11			
	12			
	13			
	14		Bn marched from MONTENESCOURT to AUBIGNY and entrained for ESQUELBECQUE.	
	15		Bn marched to DIGGERS CAPELLE area where they were billeted.	
	16		Bn in billets at DIGGERS CAPELLE	
	17		Bn marched to ARDEKE. Entrained and detrained at PROVEN. Bn to camp at PROVEN in P. area.	
	18		Bn marched to H camp near WEESTEN.	
	19		Bn proceeded to the line and relieved the 17th L.F's in the front line NE of KOEKWIT. G.H.Q at VEE BEND Relief completed without incident	
	20		Bn in front line. Intense artillery activity - Gas shells fell from 1 - 3 a.m.	

WAR DIARY / INTELLIGENCE SUMMARY

Army Form C. 2118.

Place	Date	Hour	Summary of Events and Information	Remarks and references to Appendices
	Oct	21	Bn. relieved night of 20/21 by 23rd Lancashire Fus. 27th Bn. L. Cheshires and proceed to EMILIE CAMP near ELVERDINGHE. Relief completed without incident.	
		22	Bn. in camp at EMILIE CAMP near ELVERDINGHE.	
		23	Bn. in camp at 1pm to had. B. moved to 15 MOOD east of BOESINGHE. Relieving orders at 1pm to had. B. moved to 15 MOOD east of BOESINGHE and advanced thro HOUTHULST FOREST and relieved 15th Cheshires & 15th Sherwoods (39th Div) Relief was heavy shelled & suffered [losses]. Bn. in touch with French on left flank.	
		24	Bn. in Front line. German counter attack at 5pm successfully driven off	
		25		
		26	Bn. relieved by 9th Lincolns and moved by rail from BOESINGHE to PROVEN. Arrived at PROVEN 5.15am 28/10/17 and marched to PALMA CAMP.	
		27	From Oct 23 – 27 Casualties estimates 120 & 220	
		28	110 & 220 Sick	
		29	Bn. in camp at PROVEN. Cleaning up [re-fitting]	
		30	Bn. moved by rail from PROVEN to ONDAND STATION & proceeds to DYKES CAMP. Bn in billets at DYKES CAMP	
		31	Bn. in billets at DYKES CAMP.	

R.B. [Richards] Lt Col
Capt. [illegible]

3/11/17

Appendix to WAR DIARY.

Appendix 1.   Draft of 210 OR arrived from the
8.10.17.   ~~Base~~ 11th Durham LI

Appendix 2   Draft of 3 casuals arrived
15-10-17   from the Base

Appendix 4   2/Lt B Fish 6th Border Regt reported
29.10.17.   for duty taken on strength &
               posted to "X" Co.

~~Appendix~~   Draft of 5 OR arrived from
               Base.

Appendix 5   Lt Colonel W. B. Greenwell ~~admitted~~
31·10·17   Gassed 20/10/17 but with Battalion
               until 31·10·17.

                                R B Middleton
                                Captain & Adjt
                                19th Durham LI

3   11·17

Army Form C. 2118.

WAR DIARY

INTELLIGENCE SUMMARY of the 19th (S) Bn.
The Durham Light Infantry

Vol 22

(Erase heading not required.)

Place	Date 1917	Hour	Summary of Events and Information	Remarks and references to Appendices
	Nov.	1	Bn. relieved the 15th Cheshires in support W & X Coys proceeding to KOEKUIT. Y & Z Coys. & Bn. H.Q. 6 WIJENDRIFT. Relief completed without incident. Major Huffam in Command.	
		2	Bn. in support KOEKUIT & WIJENDRIFT. Intermittent shelling both posts during day. WIJENDRIFT heavily shelled with gas shells night of 2nd/3rd. Atmospheric conditions unfavourable. Light wind.	
		3	Do. Do. gas shelling. Heavy casualties from gas shelling. Y & Z Coys. similar atmospheric conditions WIJENDRIFT again subjected to heavy gas shelling.	
		4	Bn. relieved by 7" ESSEX 53rd Bde. Relief completed by 8.30 p.m. Bn. proceeded by train from BOESINGHE to PROVEN.	
		5	Bn. in Camp at PROVEN. Camp No 4.	
		6,7	Do.	
		8	moved to P3 Camp. PROVEN. Major V.B Cookson. 19th H.L.I. took over Command.	
		9,10,11,12,13	Bn. in camp. P.3. Camp. Work improving Camp. building protectionwalls round tents &c.	
		14	Bn. moved to No 5 Camp. SIEGE CAMP. Proceeding by train from PROVEN to ELVERDINGHE.	
		15	" No. 5 SIEGE CAMP.	
		16	" relieved 17. R.Scots W. X. & Z Co. at KEMPTON PARK. Y Co. in PHEASANT TRENCH. Relief completed without incident.	
		17	" H. X. & Z Coys. at KEMPTON PARK. Y Co. in PHEASANT TRENCH	
		18	" relieved 17. R.Scots in front line. POELCAPPELLE Sector. Left Co. "W". H.Q. GLOSTER Ho. Centre Co. "Z". H.Q. POELCAPPELLE EAST. Left Co. "W". H.Q. THE BREWERY. Support Coy. "Y". (2 Platoons Y to attached W.Coy, 2. 11 & 12 attached Y Co.) Relief completed 11.30 p.m without incident.	

Army Form C. 2118.

WAR DIARY
INTELLIGENCE SUMMARY (Cont'd)
(Erase heading not required.)

Instructions regarding War Diaries and Intelligence Summaries are contained in F. S. Regs., Part II. and the Staff Manual respectively. Title Pages will be prepared in manuscript.

Place	Date	Hour	Summary of Events and Information	Remarks and references to Appendices
	Nov 1917			
	19		Bn. in front line. Left Bn. POELCAPPELLE Sector. Enemy Patrol approached about 6 a.m. Prisoners were captured and remainder of patrol believed to have been wiped out.	
	20		Bn. in front line during the day. Hostile shelling continued throughout the day. Bn. relieved by 18th LANC. FUS. and proceeded to SIEGE CAMP. HQ & X Co. to No 4 Camp. W.Y. & Z. Cos. in No. 5 Camp. Relief completed 9.30 pm. Y Co. suffered casualties coming out.	
	21		Bn. at SIEGE CAMP.	
	22			
	23		Do.	
	24			
	25		Musketry training and Range Practice.	
	26		Work on improving Camp.	
	27			
	28		Bn. relieved the 1/4th Glos. in reserve. HQ at CANAL BANK. Remainder at KEMPTON PARK. under Lt HEATON with one officer per Co. to supply R.A. & R.E. working parties. Total strength 225 OR.	
	29		As above.	
	30		Do. Heavy hostile shelling of billets at KEMPTON PARK. 6.30 a.m. to 8.15 a.m. No casualties.	

W.S. Reeve Lt A/Major
19 DF 9
3/12/17

WAR DIARY
APPENDIX.

Appendix 1.
11-12-16.   Draft of 5 casuals reported from Base.

Appendix 2.
18-12-16.   Major W.B.Greenwell reported for duty from 1st D.L.I.

Appendix 3.
24-12-16.   Draft of 163 other ranks reported from Base.

Appendix 4.
26-12-16.   2/Lieut R.Law transferred to Royal Flying Corps.

Appendix 5.
31-12-16.   Draft of 18 casuals reported from Base.

R M Middleton
2nd Lieut & Adjutant.
19th Durham Light Infantry.

APPENDIX VI.

During the 19th November 1917, 8 unwounded and 1 wounded prisoner (who subsequently died) were captured on the Battalion front.

The following extract is taken from the report of 2/Lt. R. SMITH, "X" Company, who was in charge of the left half-company front, H.Q., TRACAS FARM.

"On the morning of the 19th, a strong Officer patrol approached the Pill-box on the right flank front line, situate SPRIET MAP - EDITION 2, V.21.c.0.6. - where Pte PINKNEY was on duty as sentry to No. 5 Platoon, holding the centre post of our line. At 5.15 a.m. he challenged the enemy, who opened fire. He immediately fired and killed one of the enemy, and on a brisk fire being opened, the enemy withdrew. They were again led by their Officer round the rear of the Pill-box, right up to the centre post. Pte Pinkney again challenged and the enemy officer replied, in English, "Oh, it's alright". Pte Pinkney, however, noticing his soft cap, immediately called to the platoon and fired, killing the Officer, and the enemy were again driven off. Later in the day, the enemy patrol was completely wiped out, leaving 12 dead and 6 prisoners."

During the same morning the centre company, "Z", at MEUNIER HOUSE, observed a strong enemy patrol estimated at about 30, which was dispersed by Machine Gun and Lewis Gun fire.

In the afternoon, 4 prisoners were captured by "W" Company. The following is a copy of the report rendered by CAPT. F.MOORE, with reference to the capture.

"At 3.35 p.m. a party of Germans estimated ar four (perhaps six) was seen approaching our left platoon post (HERMES HOUSE). They had come from Pill-box V.14.b.9½.0½. On approaching, they noticed the Machine Gun on the right of our post, and halted behind two tree stumps, pointing to it. Corporal COYLE covered one of the men with his rifle. When they saw him they turned to run away. He fired, one dropped, another put his hands up and advanced to our left post, where he was taken prisoner. The other two ran southwards, and in passing our right post at NOBLES FARM, were again covered and challenged, upon which they put up their hands, came in and were made prisoners. Meanwhile Corporal Coyle and some men had gone out after these Germans. They brought in the wounded German, who was attended to by our Stretcher-bearers at centre post, but died on his way to Field Dressing Station."

W.D.Reeve. Lt +a/Adjt
19 D.L.I.

4/12/7

Appendix 5 19/20.11.17	Casualties 1 Other Ranks. Three of these on relief on night of 20th.
Appendix 6 19.11.17	See attached.
Appendix 7 21.11.17	2Lt. T.W. Harris joined from Base 2Lt. R.E. Moore-Harvey " " 2Lt. W.G. Hayman " " 2Lt. W. Partridge " " 2Lt. H.V. Tyler " "
Appendix 8 22.11.17	Capt. T. Moore to Hospital Sick.
Appendix 9 25.11.17	2Lt. R. Hall joined from Base
Appendix 10	Reinforcements 20. O.R. during the month.

W.S. Reeve.

3/12/17.

Lieut. & A/Adjt.
19th D.L.I.

Army Form C. 2118.

WAR DIARY
or
INTELLIGENCE SUMMARY of the 19th (S). Bn. The Durham Light Infantry.

1st to 31st DECEMBER 1917. (Erase heading not required.)

Instructions regarding War Diaries and Intelligence Summaries are contained in F.S. Regs., Part II. and the Staff Manual respectively. Title Pages will be prepared in manuscript.

Place	Date 1917	Hour	Summary of Events and Information	Remarks and references to Appendices
	Dec 1.		Bn. in reserve H.Q. at CANAL BANK. Remainder of Bn. at KEMPTON PARK under Lt. HEATON with 1 Off. for Coy. 6 supply RAV-RE working parties consisting of 225. O.R.	
	2.		Working party of 220. O.R. under Capt. H. SMITH remain at KEMPTON PARK for work under the C.R.E. Remainder of Bn. moved to D Camp. Sheet 28 A.30. B0.2. Relief completed at 3.30 p.m.	
	3.		30. O.R. sent up to KEMPTON PARK to reinforce Capt. SMITH'S working party.	
	4.		Bn. H.Q. moved from D Camp to KEMPTON PARK and Bn. came at Tactical disposal of 104th Inf. Bde.	
	5.		Lieut. Colonel W.B. GREENWELL rejoined from hospital and resumed command	
	6.		Major V.F. GOODERSON left to rejoin 18th H.L.I. — Details moved from D. Camp to CARIBOU CAMP Bn/pronde RE working party of 200 O.R. — Bn. under Tactical disposal of 105th Infantry Brigade.	
	7.		KEMPTON PARK — working parties.	
	8.		— do —	
	9.		Relieved by 17th Infantry Bde — Bn. joined details at CARIBOU CAMP.	
	10.		CARIBOU CAMP. — Bathing & Cleaning up.	
	11.		Bn. moved to TOAD CAMP. Sheet 27 F.25 C.8.d. — move completed by 11.30 a.m.	
	12.		TOAD CAMP. — Training & Recreation	
	13.		— do —	
	14/6 31.		— do — Major General C.M. FRANKS, C.B. inspected billets.	

W B Greenwell
Lieut. Colonel
Commanding 19th (S) Bn. Durham L.I.

2449 Wt. W14957/Mgo 750,000 1/16 J.B.C. & A. Forms/C.2118/12.

APPENDIX to WAR DIARY

Appendix 1. Capt. J.L. Waller to England.
1.11.17.

Appendix 2. Casualties — Officers 16.
1st to 4th/11/17 O.Rks. 125 (approx) of these 110
                  were gassed.
         2Lt. G.M. Allan wounded   2.11.17
         Major J. Huffam gassed   3.11.17
         2Lt. R.A. Edgar   "   "
         2Lt. R.C.J. Allan   "   "
         Capt. H.G. Rice   "   "
           (R.A.M.C.)
         2Lt. N. Wharton   "   "
         2Lt. C.E. Brown   "   "
         Capt. J.G. Ryall   "   "
         2Lt. C. Pugh   "   "
         Capt. C.B. Pearson   "   "
         Capt. L.J. Oliver   "   4.11.17
         " & adjt. R.M. Middleton "   "
         2Lt. G.K. Prior   "   "
         2Lt. R.W. Wright   "   to Hspl 5.11.17
         2Lt. E. Milner   "   do
         2Lt. R.J. Boutflower   "   to Hspl 7.11.17

Appendix 3. Major V.E. Gooderson (18th H.L.I)
8.11.17   took command
Appendix 4. Lieut J.L. Nash joined Bn from Base
9.11.17   2Lt. J. Best   — do.

WAR DIARY or INTELLIGENCE SUMMARY

Army Form C. 2118.

of 1/5 19th (S) Bn
The Durham Infantry

Place	Date	Hour	Summary of Events and Information	Remarks and references to Appendices
	Jan 1918	1st	Battalion in ROAD CAMP. Sheet 27. F.25. c.4.d. Training and Recreation	
		2	do.	
		3	do. 3 Divisional Kernel at Arm.	
		4	do.	
		5	do. Major General G.M. FRANKS. C.B. inspected transport.	
		6	do.	
		7	do.	
		8	Battalion relieved 6 London Regt. 58 Division in Canal Bank Area, moving from PROVEN to BOESINGHE by train. HQ, Y & Z Coys at TURCO HUTS, Sheet 28 NW. C15 c.1, W and X Coys at WILSONS FARM, attached to 255th Tunnelling Co. Sheet 28 NW. C26 d.5.1. QM Stores & Details at RED CHATEAU & WHITE MILL CAMP Sheet 28t B15 c.2.8. Transport lines BRIDGE CAMP Sheet 28 B20 b.	
		9th	H.Q, Y & Z Co. at TURCO HUTS available for working parties for R.E. 1/9th NF (Pioneers). W & X Coys at WILSONS FARM attached to 255th Tunnelling Co. R.E.	
		10th	Inspection ? on g? 26 O.R. attached to 205th Field C.T.E at CALIFORNIA FORT while Brigade in forward area.	
		11th	do.	
		12th	do.	
		13th	do. Lt. Col. W.B. GREENWELL D.S.O. took over command 106th INF BDE.	
		14	Major C.W. HOWES in Command of Battalion	
		15	do.	
		16	HQ, Y & Z Co. moved from TURCO HUTS to BRIDGE CAMP No.1 Sheet 28 B20 b. W & X Coys at WILSONS FARM	
		17th	do.	
		18	W & X Co. relieved at WILSONS FARM & joined remainder of Battalion at BRIDGE CAMP	
		19	Battalion at BRIDGE CAMP	
		20	do.	

WAR DIARY (Continued)
INTELLIGENCE SUMMARY

Army Form C. 2118.

Place	Date	Hour	Summary of Events and Information	Remarks and references to Appendices
	Jan 21st 1918		Battn relieved 12th ROYAL SUSSEX REGT (39th Division) in WESTROOSEBEKE Sector. Right Bn Front. H.Q. MONTPRINZ FARM. Sheet 28 N.E. D.3. C.50.45. W Coy (O.C. Lieut HAUGH) Left Front, 8 Posts V.28. b.2.7 X Coy (O.C. Capt. H. SMITH) Right Front 10 posts. Sheet 20 SE 3. V.28 & V.29 a. centrals V.29. a. 70-71. Z Coy (O.C. Capt H. HEATON MC) in support next & about VARLET FARM. Y Coy (O.C. Lieut JOPLING MC) in reserve ALBATROSS FARM. (1 Platoon INCH HOUSES) Relief complete by 8.15 pm without incident.	
	22nd		Disposition as on 21st.	
	23rd		Inter Battalion Relief. 3 Coy exchanged with W Coy. Y Coy exchanged with X Coy. 10 Officers (2Lt. CAFOX) & 27 O.R. from detail Camp. B moved to HILLTOP CAMP with Brigade training party.	
	24th		Y & 3 Coy in frontline. X Coy in Reserve. W Coy in Support.	
	25th		Bn relieved by 4th N. STAFFORDSHIRE REGT & moved into Brigade reserve at HILLTOP CAMP. Sheet 28 NW. C.21. d. Relief complete by 8.15 pm without incident.	
	26th		BN in HILLTOP CAMP. Working parties under the C.R.E.	
	27th		do	
	28th		do	
	29th		Bn relieved 17th ROYAL SCOTS in POELCAPPELLE Sector. Bn H.Q. HUBNER FARM Sheet 28 NE. Centre Coy W Coy (O.C. Lieut MAUGH) Right Front (6 posts) & BRAY FARM, BANFF HO. & VACHER FARM. Y Co: (O.C. Lieut JOPLING) Left Front (6 posts) & SHAFT, OXFORD HOUSE & unnamed Pill Box. X Co: (O.C. Capt. SMITH) Left Front (6 posts) & BERKS HOUSES + BURNS HOUSES. Z Co: (O.C. Capt. HEATON) Reserve WINCHESTER FARM. 1 Platoon INCH HOUSES. Night-post TERRIER FARM. Relief completed without incident 9.45 pm.	
	30th		Disposition as on 29th. 1 Platoon from Z Co. at INCH HOUSES relieved by 4th WORCESTERS & rejoined Company at WINCHESTER HOUSE at 1.30 AM on 31st.	
	31st		Disposition as above.	

C.J.Forster Major
Commanding 1/4 Durham L.I.